Straight Talk About Planning Your Succession

A Primer for CEOs

Abby Donnelly

THE *Leadership & Legacy* GROUP

Praise for *Straight Talk!*

"Abby has an excellent understanding of the small to mid-size business owner. She has spent years listening and understanding their wants, desires and needs. Her ability to take that knowledge and succinctly provide insightful advice has created a "must read" for anyone who is thinking about selling their business."

Adam Duggins, Managing Partner, New Page Capital

"*Straight Talk About Planning Your Succession* should be on the must-read list for any business owner. Most of the information on succession planning focuses on the financial aspects and ignores the behavioral or emotional hurdles – which can be the most difficult. I applaud Abby for giving business owners a roadmap for navigating these challenges."

Darlene Leonard, Managing Partner, Smith Leonard PLLC

"*Straight Talk!* is the perfect book for owners of small to medium size businesses who want to make the perfect exit. The Donnelly Method for Succession and Exit is a special, tried and true process to ensure a smooth and successful exit. It is very easy to read and implement. Considering all the effort you've put into your business, this book will help you get everything out of it and more!"

Henry Hutcheson, President, Family Business USA, Author,
Dirty Little Secrets of Family Business

"Abby Donnelly has written a must-read primer for anyone considering selling or transitioning a business. This book has practical, no-nonsense advice that every business owner should consume and master."

Dennis Stearns, President, Stearns Financial,
Award-winning entrepreneur and Business Scenario Planner

"After more than 30 years serving companies as a banker and now as the Chairman of the Wake Forest University Center for Private Business, I have often told Business Owners that "You are perfectly organized to get the results that you get!" *Straight Talk!* is an authentic, straightforward and insightful look at getting organized to transition your business. Abby's thoughtful and practical advice gets to the heart of what must be embraced by leaders who have the awesome responsibility to successfully transition their company on behalf of their employees, families, customers and communities."

Stanhope Kelly, Chairman,
Wake Forest University Center for Private Business

"Exiting a business that you have grown from birth to maturity is not easy. As one who has stumbled through the process of "retiring" from my own business, I have great appreciation for the methodology developed by Abby in this exit guide for business owners. In this easy and quick read, there are jewels of insight and wisdom, worthy of frequent review and reference. *Straight Talk!* spells out the preparation, planning, and execution of this difficult and emotional process. It will benefit me greatly as I bring my exit strategy to fruition, and it will be a great tool for the senior management team that now runs the company."

Steve Bright, CEO, Bright Plastics

"For nearly two decades, Abby has been transforming the way business owners think, achieve and maintain success. *Straight Talk!* serves as a compelling, natural transition for the next step of ownership…when it's time to gracefully and productively exit with purpose. Whether your exit is in five years or ten, planting the seed in your head now and following Abby's guidelines will help it feel less like an upheaval and more like the healthy, natural progression it should be."

M. Steve Cavanaugh, Jr., P.E. – President/CEO,
Cavanaugh & Associates, P.A.

THE *Leadership & Legacy* GROUP

"What makes for a successful exit? In the poem "Late Fragments", Raymond Carver asks: "And did you get what you wanted out of life, even so?" This question gets to the essence of *Straight Talk!* Abby clearly defines the necessary steps, tools and tactics to create a smooth transition, maximize the value of your business, and preserve your legacy. Straight Talk! is a must-read for any business owner and provides real value regardless of the stage of your career. Abby combines 25 years of coaching experience, with owning and selling a business, to create a roadmap to ensure business owners are able to say "yes, I did get what I wanted out of life".

Gary Fly, President, Performance CXO

"*Straight Talk!* takes succession planning from "I will think about this someday" – to — "I need to start planning now in order to do this right". Abby has spelled out the many struggles that come with exit planning, and provides the critical reasons to not delay. As a CPA and a Certified Valuation Analyst that has consulted on over 100 effective business successions, I have seen firsthand the success business owners have when they plan well — and the trials they go through when they don't. If you want to maximize the effectiveness of your exit, take a cue from the pages of *Straight Talk!*"

Duane Tolander, CPA/ABV CVA, HDH Advisors, LLC

"For any of my counterparts who own or lead a business Abby's insight and experience is extremely valuable. Her grasp of the challenges: financial, organizational, and emotional of selling your business is impressive. She speaks to the business owner as a friend facing a major life change, which is exactly what this is. The use of stories and scenarios help the business owner feel understood. Abby really strikes a chord when she relates to the sale of a home and the preparation that goes into that process. Whether you've given it any thought, or are just curious as to your next steps for your business this is a must read."

Ollie Chandhok, Market President & Publisher
Triad Business Journal

Straight Talk About Planning Your Succession: A Primer For CEOs
Abby Donnelly. – First edition
ISBN 978-0-9825078-3-4

Printed in the United States of America
FIRST EDITION

THE *Leadership & Legacy* GROUP

ACKNOWLEDGMENTS

I want to thank the following people for their support in bringing this book to fruition.

My husband, Jim Donnelly, who continues to encourage and support me as I pursue my passion, developing leaders, facilitating executive career transitions, and building meaningful relationships. I love you.

Dennis Stearns, of Stearns Financial Group, a highly respected futurist who has a talent for integrating business and economic trends into a compelling picture. His fingerprint can be found in the pages of this book.

Mark Tosczak, of Flying Car Communications, a very talented marketing expert, who has been a steady drumbeat of encouragement and a sounding board for writing a book that people might actually invest in and read.

Ann Zuraw of Zuraw Financial Advisors, a brilliant financial advisor and a very good friend who shares in my deep desire to make a difference and offer profound value, and inspires me daily to pursue my biggest hairiest goals!

Crystal Staley, Crystallized Creative, an incredibly gifted designer who consistently translates my fuzzy concepts into clear, concise and visually appealing designs. Your work is stunning.

Kevonna Hayes, my Marketing/Communications Coordinator and full time graduate student at High Point University, one of the most professional, hard-working and grounded young professionals I've had the pleasure of working with. Thank you for investing in me and LLG.

Henry DeVries and Denise Montgomery of Indie Publishing International, who took my typewritten chapters and turned them into a publishable manuscript. Henry's ability to organize and frame the content and Denise's editing expertise was invaluable.

Jed Dunn, Gary Fly, Darlene Leonard, Cindy Thompson, Brad Morton, and Dave Smith, my good friends and exceptional trusted advisors, who consistently offer me profound wisdom, great advice and hearty laughs. Each are so valuable to me! Thank you!

The fifty plus CEOs and business owners who granted me interviews as I did research for this book. Your insights and perspective clarified, validated and shaped my theories and provided direction for building the strategies and models.

I am also grateful for the many leaders who invited me into their business and life and worked with me as their CEO Coach and Trusted Advisor. It has been a joy to work with you, developing your leaders, navigating your succession, and discovering your meaningful and rewarding Next Chapter.

I celebrate you and your success!

TABLE OF CONTENTS

INTRODUCTION

Millions of owners are likely to exit their business over the next ten years as a function of aging baby boomer demographics. This will create significant economic, financial and emotional implications. Our objective is to help you prepare for the inevitable challenges—and opportunities—that come with a transition of this magnitude.

Why should you care? Because you will exit your business one day. And most business owners will require—or desire—some payout from their years of hard work to fund their retirement or to enjoy the fruits of their hard-earned return on investment. And if you don't find a qualified buyer or successor, at a sufficient valuation, those funds will not materialize, and there is a significant risk that your business will falter.

What We Will Not Cover in This Book

We are not going to get into the intricacies of business valuations, financing, negotiating, or selling your business. There are many competent professionals who can help you in those areas and we recommend engaging them at the right time.

Our goal?

We want to help you exit well and get what you want from your hard-earned years of investment in the business. There are three critical areas to craft a successful exit, and they may not be what you think. Most owners focus on the financials. Sure, those are important, but not critical.

What's critical:

- **Handling Your Emotions**
  Don't worry; this is not going to be some woo-woo new age-y

psychology book. The reality, though, is that a change of this magnitude is fraught with uncertainty and stress. Managing your emotions is the single biggest factor in ensuring you get a successful succession and exit.

- **Preparing Your Key People**
  Whether you sell to a third party or sell to a key employee or family member, your key people need to be capable of running the business profitably and sustainably.

- **Preparing Your Business—Strategy and Systems**
  A great growth strategy is only as good as the people you have executing it. If they can't bring it to fruition, you either need new people or you need a new strategy.

  The systems that are fundamental to your business need to be efficient and effective and designed for growth and flexibility. Your business will look different in the future, so your systems need to be designed to adapt to those changes.

- **Exiting Well**
  If you don't have something compelling to go *to* before you leave the business—or before you ramp down substantially—you will either muck up the business or you will come face-to-face with boredom, irrelevance, disconnection.

If we can help you avoid the risks and thrive through the process, we will consider this book a success.

A warning: The exit strategy planning process will inevitably create fear, anxiety, discomfort, and stress. And you know what? That's good. That means you are ready. We know that you have all of the wisdom and experience you need to move through it, and now you have a guide to lead you every step of the way. (If you have no fear or discomfort, you are probably not ready to embark on this journey with serious intent.)

Are you still with us? Are you sure?

I have been working with business owners of small and medium-sized businesses for more than fifteen years. I've seen the best-laid plans derail and talented owners miss opportunity. I've interviewed more than fifty owners and CEOs, read countless articles, white papers, research studies, and blogs, and what I've found is that most business owners recognize that doing this work at least three to five years before you plan to transition out of your business is critical...for someone else. There is plenty of time left for them.

Until there isn't.

When your health forces you to make a change, when your family situation shifts, when the economy takes a dive and you don't have the financial means or the energy to weather the storm...again. When you just can't stand another year of working at this intensity. Then, there is no longer time.

Well, if you are still reading, you are one of the few who is willing to admit—at least to yourself—that it is worth investing some time in now and you will reap the rewards as your business benefits, your valuation increases, and your true enthusiasm for the next twenty or more years of your life grows exponentially as you can truly begin to live the life of your dreams.

So if you are still with us, let's get started.

Why The Exit Strategy Planning Process Won't Work for You

There is often much anticipation and hope when starting a new project or building a new habit. As business owners, you are driven to succeed, and getting on board with a new program, strategy, or direction can be exciting.

As the work continues, you will, like many hard-driving successful owners, move past the excitement stage and find yourself facing *the challenge of implementation.* Your energy will wane; your frustration will mount. Results are not flowing (at least not yet) and boredom has set in. That is going to happen here, as well, unless you do two critical things:

1. **Find a partner, preferably one with a complementary skill set to you**, whom you can trust with personal information and some "not-for-public-knowledge" information about your business. This person won't need to read your P&L or know your compensation, but might need to be a sounding board for conversations about your executive team or board. The partner could be a:

   - Business colleague who is going through a similar transition.
   - Key employee or family member who meets the criteria.
   - Previous mentor
   - An organization like Vistage International, Women Presidents' Organization, The Alternative Board, or C12
   - A hired executive coach who has expertise working with the C-suite, preferably with exposure to succession and exit.

   Tell your partner what you are embarking upon and ask if he or she would be willing to commit about two to three hours each month to work on this with you.

   Your partner will be a valuable asset as you move through the book and complete the exercises.

2. **Make a commitment to yourself to face reality.** Harsh? Yes, but this is tough stuff. It's hard work and it will not be any easier if you choose to ignore or deny reality. You will need to be self-aware, which means owning up to your strengths and weaknesses. And sometimes owning up to strengths is harder! You will need to look at your business through the lens of a buyer, with a "what's in it for a buyer" mentality. You are going to have to admit fear, anxiety, discomfort, and stress—at least to yourself. This is the harsh reality.

Here is what we see going on in the marketplace and the specific implications for business owners financially, mentally, and (I dare say) emotionally.

Notes:

THE *Leadership & Legacy* GROUP

SECTION I:
Why Plan Your Exit Now?

CHAPTER 1:

What's Keeping You from Planning Your Exit Right Now?

Nearly 90 percent of owners recognize the need for a succession plan, but only 10 percent have a written plan in place.[1] That's not surprising, since this is a new experience for many owners. Seventy-five percent of owners have never tried to exit a business.[2]

For most owners, exiting a business you've poured your heart and soul into can be very difficult and since most owners don't have an external deadline, the timing is completely up to you. In many cases, there is no real sense of urgency— until there is. Whether you are 55, 60, or 70, you decide when. So, if you don't get started with a plan this year, there is always next year. It's easy to put off another year until one year becomes ten, and there is still no plan.

This is what Patrick Ungashick, author of *Dance in the End Zone*, has called "The Rolling Ten."[3] Ask an owner when they plan to exit their business; most will answer, "five to ten years." Ask again in three to five years and most will answer, "five to ten years." Ask again in three to five years and you get the point. You really never have to start planning, because five years is certainly ample time to figure this out, right? In fact, 60 percent of owners have delayed their exit plan.[4]

Sure; health issues, family dynamics, a spouse who wants to travel, a sudden offer to buy your business, or just finally admitting you're worn out can put urgency into your timeline, but often there is no defined date by which the exit must occur. That's the good news. The bad news is that *there is no defined date by which the exit must occur.*

And probably no big surprise, most owners' identities are deeply entrenched in their business. Owners are used to being the owner—the top dog! Employees listen to the owner. They have to, or their jobs are on the line. Walking away from your business, even with the luxury of a strong sale value, means you walk away from the status, the control, and the reputation that come with being an owner. And you'll have to redefine many of the relationships in your life. They've been defined in the context of you as "The Owner." Redefining those relationships can be difficult because the reason for them existing has either changed or gone away.

You may recall times when employees you really liked left your business on good terms. You both committed to keeping in touch and you meant it. But months go by and you didn't talk. If you did connect, it was friendly and nice, but the energy and passion you once shared around common goals were gone. Well, the same will happen here, only worse. Your status will change as you go from "The Owner" to "Someone Who Used to Be Someone."

So, if there is not something meaningful, compelling, and rewarding to go to, why leave? If you stay, you get to keep your top-dog status, bring home a paycheck, profit from the thrill of running the business, and you don't need to deal with the discomfort of financial, strategic, or exit challenges. It's more comfortable to stay with the familiar, with what you know.

Intellectually, we can justify staying as a better use of our time, or better for the business, or a way to continue the income stream. Emotionally, this can get in the way of good business decisions and effective leadership. As you disengage from or tire of the rigor it takes to run and grow a business, your business will suffer.

The level of uncertainty involved in the exit planning process, and the lack of experience most owners have in selling a business, makes it easy to postpone the hard work of planning succession and exit.

Potential Emotional Exit Challenges

❏ I need to let my leaders run the business, but I have a hard time letting go. I've invested years in this business. It's hard to leave and risk seeing the organization change direction or struggle.

❏ I am not quite ready to trust my successor(s) to run the business.

❏ This business is my legacy. I want to make sure it lives on forever.

❏ I am stressed out about how to exit the business gracefully. I need something to really look forward to but I'm uncomfortable admitting I don't know what that is.

❏ I don't know how to figure out what will be meaningful.

❏ I'm anxious about missing the challenge of running a business—being in charge.

❏ I am concerned about going from 60 hours to zero hours per week overnight.

❏ I wonder how many "good years" I still have left, and realize time is running out.

❏ I worry a bit about losing my identity, my status. Who am I without my role in this company?

❏ I am concerned about plunging into insignificance. "Nobody listens to me anymore."

❏ What if I go soft, lose my edge, get really bored, have no direction after I sell my business?

❏ I'm worried about the impact of such a major change in routine and life habits and patterns.

❏ My spouse and I are both anxious about the impact this change will have on our marriage, family, self-image, and health.

❏ The truth is that I'm tired, burned out, ready to slow down—and maybe feeling a little guilty about it.

TOTAL: _____

How did you do? If you're like most business owners, you probably saw some truth in several focus areas, but one or two areas concern you most. You may also have recognized challenges that are not listed above.

Write down your top 2 here:

_____

_____

This set of common problems is tricky to interpret. Your answers may indicate you need to build more confidence in your management team before you are ready to exit. You may not feel that they can run the business profitably and sustainably without you—yet. In fact, according to a 2014 Business Enterprise Institute Business Owner Survey Report, 85 percent of business owners looking to make a transition from their business do not have someone who can replace their skills and/or responsibilities.[2] If you did, you might find it easier to exit. (If that is your true challenge, chapters 6 and 7 will be of great value to you.)

Though confidence in your management team may be the most commonly stated issue, often the real issue is that you are uncertain about who you are and what you will do if you don't have this business to run. There is no shame in feeling this way; most owners do. They just don't admit it (sometimes even to themselves). If you think there is even a remote possibility that this may be true for you, you need to address it, or you will create unnecessary stress and risk in your business. (You need to do the personal work outlined in Section III.)

Don't let your emotions get in the way
of building a strong management team that can truly
run your business profitably and sustainably.

CHAPTER 2:

You're Not Guaranteed a Win: Competing in a Buyer's Market

Financial Considerations

With an estimated 4.5 million businesses changing hands in the next ten years[5] as boomers age out and exit, this wave of acquisitions, multi-generational successions, and sadly—in many cases—liquidations will create a massive buyer's market, lowering the value of each business and creating a ripple of stress and uncertainty as owners, C-suite leaders and employees at all levels worry. Owners will worry about funding their retirement and the sustainability of their business. C-suite leaders may want the top job and worry they won't get it. Everyone will wonder whether they will have a job, or get along with the new owners, or if the business can even survive and thrive under new management.

Since over 65 percent of employees in business are employed at small to medium-sized businesses[6] that ripple of stress and uncertainty will impact a critical mass of people, all across our local economy.

If you just wait, hoping everything will work out, well, you might get lucky and it will. More likely, you will find yourself caught in the midst of this tsunami, and the results could be devastating.

Financial Risks

This financial challenges assessment will help you more fully identify the financial focus areas you'll need to address in the Exit Strategy Planning process. Check all that apply.

Common Financial Challenges: Funding a Retirement Lifestyle

❑ I'm worried I won't have enough money to maintain my lifestyle after exit.

❑ I am frustrated that I have continually reinvested in the business and there may not be a return on investment for me.

❑ I am disappointed that the value of my business is not a lot higher.

❑ I am annoyed that I have to work so hard *on* the business now to increase the valuation.

❑ I'm concerned I am going to have to finance the sale of my business if I can't find someone who can pay for it.

❑ Without cash from the sale of the business, I can't retire.

❑ I am uncertain of the value of my business. I always assumed it would be enough.

❑ I am anxious about selling the business in the midst of the coming tsunami, but I am not ready to sell it now.

TOTAL: _____ out of 8

How did you do? If you're like most business owners, you probably saw some truth in several focus areas, but one or two areas concern you most. You may also have recognized challenges that are not listed above.

List those below and then rank order your top financial challenge here:

_____

_____

For most business owners, the majority of their wealth—and their retirement funding—is tied up in their business[5], so they need to sell their business to fund their retirement.

The first question is not what your business is worth; it's what kind of a financial return you *need* from your business. You've spent the last twenty to forty years reinvesting in the growth of your company. Sure, you've taken a nice salary and generous perks, but you have likely not created a massive retirement fund that you are anxiously waiting to tap into. So you've got to figure out how much you need for retirement to live the lifestyle you want and what resources you already have; the difference determines what you *need* from the business.

Next, you'll need to find out if your business is worth that. A business valuation will help answer that. And before you panic, a good business valuation, done by a certified valuation expert, can cost as little as $3,000 to $5,000. This level of valuation is usually sufficient as a benchmark for most relationship sales. It's also a good starting place for owners seeking a strategic buyer. You can use this valuation to evaluate how much work you want to put into growing the value of the business or whether you should just ride it out and hope for the best. You would also know what it will take for any family member or key employee to buy your business and actually pay you out over time. Finding out the valuation gives you a starting point to begin thinking about succession and what's next.

Here is what is most perplexing: 42 percent said that maximizing business value is their number one goal[4], but 78 percent of owners have not established a formal transition advisory team[5] and likely don't know what their business is worth. In fact, only 11 percent of owners have valued their business[2]. It's hard to know if you have enough for retirement or are maximizing your value if you have no idea what it's worth. Back-of-napkin self-calculations don't count.

Some owners are not as concerned about maximizing their financial return. They want a family member or key employee(s) to buy the business from them. I call this a "relationship sale." The owners can't afford or don't want to *give* the business away. They need enough return to fund their lifestyle in retirement, but their top priority is to support a successful transition to their family member or key employees. A firm we worked with recently is proactively developing three key leaders for an ownership role in the business. Whether all three of them, two, one, or none of them will be the owner one day is yet to be determined, but the owner is making an investment in them, not only to allow for that possibility, but also to proactively increase that likelihood.

If your business is worth more than the bare minimum you need after you determine your personal financial planning goals, good for you! That means you decide what you want to get from the business and the prospective buyer decides if they will pay it. Many owners *want* to get–a lot more than they *need* from the business unless they are selling to their son, daughter, or maybe a loyal key employee.

If your business is not worth the bare minimum you need to retire on, you have some work to do and it's good that you know that now. It's going to take some time to build value into the business.

But before you breathe a sigh of relief and roll up your sleeves to add more value to your business, it's critical to recognize that the picture you just painted may work for today, but we also know from the coming tsunami that the market is going to get very competitive over the next 10 years. Unless you are going to add that value very quickly, the glut of retiring/exiting owners is going to create a buyer's market.

During that tsunami, valuations will be lower, which means your business is going to have to stand out in order to attract the serious attention of a third-party buyer. John Leonetti, the author of *Exiting Your Business, Protecting Your Wealth*[4], found that while 75 percent of business owners want to sell their business (Strategic Advisors), only 20 percent actually sell. What will it take to make yours one of those?

If you sell to a family member or key employee, it is highly likely you will have to finance the sale and position the business for sustainable growth and profitability to ensure you get paid out. Most family members and key employees are not sitting on a mountain of cash or a lot of equity to borrow against.

In addition, the risks of a sustainable second generation of business are high. Only 30 percent of businesses survive to the second generation.[7] Many that do fail to reach their financial and growth potential. It gets even worse as we look at survival into the third generation. Only 13 percent survive into the third generation, and 6 percent into fourth.[8,9]

Without sufficient funding for retirement, you will either be forced to stay on in the business or accept a reduced quality of lifestyle.

Even if an owner has sufficient funding for retirement, the likelihood of experiencing significant age-related health issues increases significantly after age 65. For owners passing the business to a family member, this can create a double whammy, as the owner and the family are deeply involved in caretaking and business operations, not to mention the rising cost of health care.

Many businesses in this situation won't get sold for anything close to fair value due to the owner having increasing difficulty managing the business. Dozens of other problems also arise after age 65, including top performers leaving because they see the writing on the wall and owners becoming less rational as they go through the challenge of selling the business.

You need to assess the value of your business, the financial requirements you have for retirement, the likely transaction value from a sale, and explore your options for actually transacting the business. Start with a valuation expert who can give you a benchmark value and a business-savvy wealth advisor who can integrate the valuation with your personal financial situation. If you don't have those resources already in your network, ask around and get recommendations.

Get the data you need to guide your next steps:
What is your business worth?
How much money do you need?

Notes:

Notes:

THE *Leadership & Legacy* GROUP

SECTION II:
How to Make Your
Succession Plan Succeed?

CHAPTER 3:

Transferring or Selling a Profitable, Sustainable Business

Let's face it; most owners have never sold a business before. Built a business? Absolutely. But the strategies, skills, and experience needed to start or build a business are very different than those needed to sell a business. Often owners confide in us that they don't even know what questions to ask or what resources to engage. In fact, only 38 percent of respondents to a Business Owner Survey think they have identified all steps necessary to successfully exit their business[2]. Where do you start? The truth is that every situation is different and brings its own level of complexity.

This strategic common problems assessment will help you identify what strategic challenges you'll need to address in this process.

Common Strategic Problems

❏ I'm uncomfortable…I've never sold a business. I don't even know where to begin.

❏ I am worried our strategy is insufficient to ensure long-term growth and profitability.

❏ I'm frustrated with our management and financial infrastructure and systems. They are ineffective and demand too much of my time.

❏ I am concerned about strategic gaps in my successor's capability and capacity.

❏ I'm anxious about finding a buyer. I can't finance the sale and my employees can't afford to buy me out.

❏ I am worried that I have not adequately prepared my management team to lead the strategy we need to maintain our competitive advantage.

❏ I am beginning to hear rumbling in the break room about succession and I don't know how to head off the rumors.

❏ I am concerned about how to transfer my skills, expertise, and business relationships.

❏ I know I need a strong management team to represent our strategic advantage to prospective buyers. I'm worried they aren't ready.

❏ I'm disappointed in our financial situation and I haven't put the resources in place to address it.

❏ My kids think they are ready to take over. They're not. It's causing tension in the family.

TOTAL: _____

How did you do? If you're like most owners, you probably saw some truth in each challenge, but one or two are of more concern for you.

Rank order your top 2 challenges below.

_____

_____

The strategic risks are a little more complex than the financial risks. If you want your business to deliver the Return-on-Investment (ROI) you need to fund your retirement, you've got two choices:

1. Create and market your unique strategic advantage and find the right third party buyer

2. Build strategic leverage in your management team

Yikes! Neither one of these sound easy. Both will take time to plan and implement. Let's look at each of these choices in more depth.

Market Your Unique Strategic Advantage

You need to stand out and clearly differentiate your business from the many small businesses that are going to be available at cut rates so you can get the strategic deal of a lifetime—or at least get a deal when others are liquidating or taking a bath. That might be easy if your business is in a unique niche or has done exceptionally well in the industry, and you are viewed as a formidable competitor. If not, as is true for most businesses, you'll need to create that differentiation, effectively communicate it, and then prove it out. But if it were that easy, most owners would have already created that differentiation.

Start with some basic strategic planning methodologies to help you uncover your unique competitive advantage. You'll need to figure out how to differentiate yourself and proactively work with a valuation expert or broker to help you evaluate what that advantage is worth, what it will take to find your strategic buyers and how to market it successfully to that audience.

Build Strategic Leverage in Your Management Team

One of the biggest issues you'll face—one that is rarely put on the table—is the risk that comes with inattention to strategy. We're not saying you haven't had a strategy—though many have not; we're saying that most owners who have invested thirty years in their business have a deep intuitive understanding of the industry, market, and economic implications that influence their business and have been able to make effective strategic adjustments over time to address, counteract, or leverage those changes. It's so intuitive that nobody else sees the change needed; certainly not as easily as you.

It's unlikely a successor will bring that same intuitive understanding or experience to bear. How will you help the successor recognize and take early advantage of economic, governmental, or industry trends to accelerate growth or position their product or service to capture a new market opportunity? How will you help him or her assess the changing competitive pressures? Many opportunities are opening up even as there are more ways for competitors from inside and outside your industry to come in and either take parts of your business away or weaken you so much in the process that your business will no longer be worth what it is today.

Without this ability to assess, it's more difficult to create opportunities for a higher-value strategic sale and may create a competitive disadvantage for your successor(s), who may then find themselves on the catch-up side of changing trends or the volatile marketplace.

On the other hand, fresh perspective from your younger employees might be exactly what your business needs right now. Technology, communications, and access to resources are changing businesses so quickly that it's possible that you are the dinosaur, and your business could benefit from a shift in strategy despite your years of industry and business experience. The exposure millennials and gen Xers have to technology and information has opened up new avenues for growth. While they may not have the wisdom to lead a multi-million-dollar business the way you do, they may bring a competitive advantage that you would never have recognized.

Even if your strategy is sound, the very real—and very practical—strategic risks include identifying and securing your successor. You need someone you can have confidence in, someone you trust, or you will never let go. Even if the business value is not a driving concern for you, it can be incredibly stressful if you don't have confidence in your successor. He or she will make changes. That's guaranteed. Your successor is not you and will not do things the way you do things, no matter how much training you've done.

Successors may slay sacred cows, reverse decisions you've made, take on new product lines, fire vendors or customers, spend more money than you expected, and on and on. Are these actions bad? Maybe. Maybe not. They will also make mistakes. You did. And so will they. But now, their mistakes are in *your* business—especially difficult if the mistakes are big. Especially difficult if you are financing the sale. So, what are you going to do? You can't run it forever. You can't consistently step on their toes or usurp their leadership. If you do, your employees will lose respect for your successor, and maybe for you, too. You have to walk a fine line between offering the successor enough guidance to ensure he or she does not fail, and not so much that you are meddling, micromanaging, or still running the business yourself.

Your employees are also watching…closely. They want to see how this transition plays out so they can make their own career decisions. Whether they applaud your selection or not, they may feel that the devil they know (you) seems better than the devil they don't (your successor). While the employees may know the new leader and have even worked with him or her successfully for many years, the new role will change the organizational dynamics. You can't afford for employees to leave or disrespect your successor, and you can't expect your demands on them to embrace the changes to work.

Hearing all of this may make it easy to put off finding a qualified successor (buyer). Whether it's a relationship sale or a third-party sale, it can take time. Lots of time. Without a successor or buyer, you have no sale, and the only viable exit becomes liquidation.

If you go the route of a strategic buyer, the key is finding a strategic buyer who can deliver the financial, cultural, and business goals you have for your company, people, and exit.

If you go the route of finding a successor, who is the right successor? Can he or she be prepared to run the business when you need it? And is the successor even interested in owning your business? Can the successor deliver the strategy, now and in the future, despite changing market conditions?

You'll need to position your business to be run profitably and sustainably under his or her leadership—your son or daughter, brother, niece or nephew, or your CFO, VP of Sales, or VP of operations.

Of course, you'll likely need to reap enough return on the profit each year to continue to build your nest egg while simultaneously figuring out a financial model that will allow you to finance your successor's dream of ultimately owning your business.

Now that you have clarity on your biggest challenges we can explore the Three Ugly Truths.

CHAPTER 4:

Dealing with the Three Ugly Truths

When we boil it all down—the financial, strategic, and emotional—we get the *big three*: the three core truths that will derail you if you don't address them.

1. **No qualified buyer (or successor), no sale.** If you have a successor who doesn't have the interest, skills, or financial resources to run your business, you don't have a sale. If you have a successor who has those, but you don't have enough confidence to truly let go, you don't have a sale. If your qualified, vetted third party buyer drops out at the eleventh hour, you don't have a sale.

2. **Your identity is deep in this business.** You can try to deny it. You can try to argue it. You can bury your head in the sand, but you will eventually recognize that this process is going to challenge you to your very core. The sense of accomplishment, satisfaction, and yes, ego that has fueled your success is right here—in this business. And by design, that is going to change.

3. **There is great discomfort in the stress and uncertainty** that comes with exiting your business. There is so much unknown and unknowable. You've dealt with stress and uncertainty successfully before, but this is the first time in a long time that you were embarking on something so complex and so different than anything you have done before. So gear up and prepare to do it again.

The *Real* Ugly Truth

The *real* reason we put off moving forward, taking those first critical steps, doing what we <u>know</u> we need to do is...*this process is emotional.* Highly emotional. And dealing with our *emotions* is hard. And dare we risk a bit of a gender stereotype and say...it's especially hard for men. Not because men don't have emotions, but because culturally, it's just not as acceptable for men, especially highly driven, 55–75-year-old *successful business-owner* men, to acknowledge and discuss these kinds of emotions.

Men pound tables and put on a brave face. Men grunt and suck it up. They analyze balance sheets and P&L's, engineer wastewater treatment systems, develop methods to revolutionize the health care industry, but they do not talk about their identities in their businesses, or the uncertainty and stress of doing something new when they are supposed to be a "got-it-all-together" seasoned business owner. Nor do they talk about the absolute abject fear of turning over their business baby to a new caregiver.

We get pushback from some men even just characterizing this root cause as "emotional." The strong recommendation was to call it "Mental Readiness," as John Leonetti does in his book. While mental readiness certainly is part of it, that term does not fully capture the experience. How do we know this? After working with boomer business owners for many, many years, I started interviewing them to learn about their succession and exit plans. Most of the people I interviewed in round one would not acknowledge these truths. Once I shared my research, most were quick to agree with it. They recognized that this process is not comfortable, and they were used to just dealing with it because they didn't have anyone to talk to about these issues.

In fact, the first twenty conversations went something like this:

> *So, have you done anything specific to prepare for your succession?*
> "Oh, yes, everything is going very well."

> *So, what kinds of things have you done?*
> "Well, I really don't need to do much to prepare for succession right now. Eventually, we'll start looking at that. I have some ideas of how I want it to go, but I have good people and I know it will all work out."

Have you identified your likely successor or buyer?
"Oh, yes, I want Mark to take over the business. He's got a natural business sense and he's been with us for 18 years. But he'll need to work closely with Melanie. She's been with us for 10 years and she's going to have to help out with sales. Mark is an engineer and really doesn't know anything about sales."

Who drives sales now?
"I do."

What are you doing to get Mark and Melanie ready to take these areas over?
"Oh, I'll eventually want to get them in front of our customers for sure, but not yet. They're not ready yet. And I'll want to make sure Mark can manage the financials. He's had his hands full just managing the operations."

This is avoidance behavior, plain and simple, and it's not going to work.

Practically everyone I spoke to was either uncomfortable facing the need for a plan or overly optimistic about the need for proactive succession planning and exit. Common responses:

- I don't want to even think about succession or exit. It's still years away.

- I don't have to do anything about this right now. Everything is fine and on track.

- My team is doing great. They'll be ready to run the company one day.

We want to stress the significance of this underlying emotional root cause. If you are not willing or able to consider the implications of both the mental and the emotional aspects of succession planning and exit, you will find this process to be much more challenging in so many surprising ways, and much less likely to deliver any meaningful financial or strategic return. You have invested too much in growing your business to risk allowing your emotions to derail the process.

CHAPTER 5:

Getting Real When Planning for Succession

When you put off succession planning, there is always an emotional component. Sure, we can talk about the legitimate challenges of finding a qualified successor and we can justify why the time isn't right to begin planning. We can even argue we have a plan...in our heads. We can tell ourselves and even our employees that we are a healthy, vibrant, and engaged 65-year-old and we plan to run the place until we're 80, but that won't stop the speculation or concern, and it certainly won't stop the reality that you need to put a qualified successor or buyer in place.

It's true that if you don't have a strong leadership team and an identified successor in place when you are ready for succession, you should prepare for tough times ahead. Could you get a Hail Mary in the fourth quarter and sell your business in a strategic sale to a buyer who has an intact leadership team that fits well with your culture, or purchases your company for a lot of money in an asset sale? Yes. It could happen. But it's unlikely.

The strength of a business is dependent on the strength of the leadership team. These high-level leaders set the vision, put management systems in place, and ensure the profitable implementation of your strategic plan.

If the business transitions to a third-party buyer, the value of the business may be heavily influenced by the quality of your leadership team. They will represent the business to those third-party prospective buyers who will often pay more if the business is strong and the owner is considered expendable. Without that, you will probably need to do an earn-out, working for someone else in your business, hoping to get a full payout.

If the business transitions to your family or key leaders, as we mentioned earlier, they will need to run it profitably and sustainably for you to get your full payout. Investing in your C-suite leaders' professional development provides an opportunity for you to reap the rewards of a stronger team *now*—*and* in the future, with a stronger purchase price when the time is right. Unfortunately, only 15 percent of business owners have hired and trained employees to take over key business responsibilities.[2]

Owners' Syndrome

While few business owners will admit this in public, most are uncomfortable—if not downright stressed out—with both the challenge of turning their business over to someone else *and* the challenge of facing the looming prospect of twenty-plus years of…*who knows what?*

Our society revels in the idea of retirement. We look longingly at those who have earned the right to live free of expectations, free of the pressure, demands, and the stress of day-to-day business responsibilities. We covet the time and opportunity to pursue new interests, to sleep in, to tackle hobbies that have lain dormant for many years. But in reality, for most business owners, the shock of moving from a full-time business leader to a life of uncertainty is very unsettling.

It's hard to get much sympathy for that as you talk to friends, neighbors, business colleagues, or those you volunteer with. And if you do happen to get sympathy, you may find yourself roped into doing volunteer work or other projects on a much more aggressive schedule than you had in mind, or end up putting your energy into someone else's long-standing priorities and goals, rather than investing in your own.

We understand. In entrepreneur circles, the term "Founder's Syndrome" describes entrepreneurs who found a business and then will not let go. The passion of the founder may limit the further growth and success of the business.

Many owners have what we call "Owner's Syndrome," an iteration of Founders Syndrome wherein the owner will not let go of the business, and their commitment to the business—or their fear of letting go—limits succession, sale, and exit. Owners need to be able to let go of the day-to-day, embrace their successor's or buyer's strategic decisions, and eventually let them own and run the business. According to a Price Waterhouse survey, 75 percent of business owners surveyed "profoundly regretted" the decision to sell.[10]

Ready for an Identity Shift?

We know that after years of living the "American Dream" of creating a successful business, many business owners' personal identities are inextricably linked to their business. It's difficult to imagine letting the business go because it's so much a part of them. Transitioning to a family member or key employee—or even a sale to a third party—can be gut-wrenching as the new owner stakes their claim and makes changes in strategy, staffing, systems, and culture. Changes may also be risky if the change does not produce the growth and profitability required.

Social Expectations: Because "retirement" is a historically coveted time in our country, the traditional response to hearing of an impending retirement is excitement for the retiree and possibly a hint of jealousy for all of the free time and flexibility this stage of life will afford that person. Statistically, most hard-charging business owners will live an additional twenty to thirty years or more in reasonably good health after traditional retirement age.

Friends drool, but for you…if you were willing to admit the truth, it may not be that enticing. Most owners are very uncomfortable with the idea of retiring and can be terrified of the prospect of long days of nothing to do. There is only so much time you can spend traveling, playing golf, and visiting family. They fear boredom, lack of meaningful involvement, loss of professional relationships and community, and becoming obsolete. And they *should* fear those. As we age, health issues naturally become a concern, so when we experience a major life change along with the potential identity shifts that can surface through a business exit, leaders can experience higher levels of anxiety, stress and other health challenges. That risk can be mitigated by intentionally building a transition plan into a meaningful

THE *Leadership & Legacy* GROUP

and rewarding next chapter. The proven process we use for partnering with business owners to define their next chapter transforms them from reluctant to engaged in their future.

Owners who struggle most with identity in their business are unwilling to develop a plan for exit because they don't see it as a viable option in the near term. They often cannot imagine life without the business, or the business functioning effectively without them—independent of the capability of their management team, which often is also insufficient to run the business.

So identity becomes a big emotional barrier.

Changing Attitudes

The parents of baby boomers often considered age 65 as a hard date for retirement and felt fortunate to live into their late 70's. That is no longer the case.

Today, while many business owners may choose to reduce the time and intensity they put into their business, they are the first generation that will enjoy twenty or more healthy years of life after age 65. There is no clear roadmap for this generation to define what life looks like after age 65, and in fact, many are rejecting the term "retirement," because they are rewriting what is possible for seniors.

In fact, most C-suite boomers who leave their business or job after age 60 do *not* want to retire. They feel they have way too much left in them to give and they want to engage with the business community and contribute to the success of an organization. And many still want to earn a paycheck. They may want to work on slightly different terms (selecting specific aspects of a role—doing just the parts they want), or to choose a different industry or role (moving from manufacturing to health care, or from for-profit to nonprofit, or from a CEO role to a CFO role). They may want to work at a different pace (thirty-five hours per week versus sixty), but they do not want to exit the workforce.

It can be extremely uncomfortable for them when others use the word "retire" to describe them because the label sends a message that can really hamper their search process. That label, by design, alters the perception others have of them, changing their reputation, shifting their credibility and altering their brand as the image of them becomes one of "retiring." Doors close or never open because people think lame duck, tired, no longer interested in contributing at a professional level, etc. Or worse, they don't think of them at all and opportunities never materialize.

That assumption is particularly hard to combat when those leaders really want to work and really are seeking employment. It makes it difficult for them to be taken seriously in a career search. This is a significant issue because many of them want to work (and have great skills and experience to bear). They need to be taken seriously to find that right fit role.

Changing this perception will help the local economy as those leaders who want to stay in the workforce can continue to add tremendous value. Spreading the word on the trend and helping those who do want to work connect with the kind of work they are looking for will go a long way toward helping them be taken seriously and helping organizations thrive.

In fact, the trend today is to avoid the use of the word retirement altogether, in favor of language such as "encore career" or "next chapter." We use the phrase "what's next?", which is the subject of our next book and a significant portion of our client work as we guide executives through a proactive and intentional process of discovery to build a meaningful and rewarding transition, whether paid or not.

The High Cost of Avoidance

Failing to properly prepare for a leadership transition or to properly deal with the emotional and personal issues associated with retirement and a business sale will scuttle its chances for success far more than poor economic conditions. Preparing the business for a high-value sale, preparing the leadership team to run and grow a profitable venture, and preparing an owner for a meaningful and rewarding "what's next" are critical to a successful succession plan. And the planning must start now. This work cannot be done overnight. Much of it will take three to five years of planning and implementation.

Putting Off Succession Planning Will Not Improve Your Ability to Manage the Inherent Uncertainty of This Process

One of the most effective ways to maintain or grow your business value is to proactively manage uncertainty. Every business faces uncertainty and risk, but if the owner is nearing retirement age, there are additional uncertainties that will come into play.

Fear and speculation about an aging owner and the potential of new ownership will happen whether you say anything about your plans or not. Your employees and customers know your approximate age. They will speculate, especially if you have any visible health concerns. You can do much to manage this by choosing behaviors and communications that are truthful and instill confidence. That does not mean that you need to share anything before you are ready, but so often owners say nothing, so rumors start and then when you do say something, your communications become suspect. Simply communicating that you are putting plans in place to secure the future of the company can buy you time and put rumors to bed…for a while. Just make sure it's true.

Speculation will have a direct impact on the organization's results— including the potential for reduced revenue as your customers worry you won't be around in the future. Turnover as your employees worry about the security of their job. Productivity and innovation as you slow down.

The reality is, your business is only as valuable as the price someone is willing and able to pay for it, but we can say that without developing a strong management team and managing the stress and uncertainty, you risk that there won't be anybody willing or able to pay what you think it's worth. Since everyone will leave their business someday, it's important that you face these ugly truths now.

We'll show you how to look at the adequacy of your strategy, building one strong enough to deliver the financial return you need. We'll show you how to evaluate the strength of your management team and build a development plan for them that will ensure you maximize their capability and potential for your business success. No matter what your timing is for an exit, wouldn't you rather have a strong, capable management team leading your business?

The Challenge of Inexperience

Business owners have a wealth of experience in their industries and a long track record of success in business. When it comes to succession planning, the sale of a business, and exit, even seasoned owners rejoin the ranks of the inexperienced. It can be difficult for this group to reach out and get the guidance they need to work through the transition. But with the help of a professional experienced in guiding businesses through the succession, sale, and exit process, owners can maximize their opportunity to achieve the financial goals they require and avoid the emotional issues that plague so many others.

So how do you position yourself to benefit from this and avoid the pitfalls and risks that are inherent in the process?

The Donnelly Method was developed to help owners navigate the succession planning and exit strategy planning process. The next chapter is focused on the six components that make up The Donnelly Method. These components can make a marked difference in how you navigate this transition.

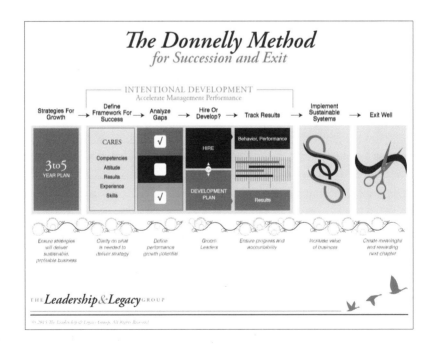

CHAPTER 6:

Ensuring Long-Term Strategic Alignment

What Do You Want from Your Business?

Seriously—what do you want from your business? What was your goal or objective when you started it ten, twenty, thirty-five years ago?

I know your tendency is to just read on. It's hard to think about what we really want—and sometimes harder to admit what we want. Society sends strong messages about what we should want—what's OK to want. Families send strong messages, too. Many owners we've worked with want a fair return on their investment and want to see the business grow and thrive through a relationship sale. Others want to maximize their shareholder return, buy a beach house, travel the world, and enjoy the fruits of their labor. Others want to stick around, work part-time, enjoy some travel, get involved in other things that they've always been too busy to do, and see the next generation grow and prosper.

I asked Harry*[11], a 60-year-old owner of an $8 million technology company, what he wanted from his business. He told me, "It would be easy to say I want to make a lot of money, but truly, I want a fair price for my business, and I want to position my loyal employees to own it one day if they are interested. I would like to stick around until I'm about 65, working part-time, financing the sale of the business to them, and see the business grow with their leadership."

What about you?

Aligning to Strategy

It's easy to get caught up in the day-to-day operations of your business. The thrill of a big sale; the fires that crop up that demand your attention and expertise; the people issues that seem to never end; these interruptions and distractions often consume our working lives. But strategy, whether derived formally or informally, intentionally or intuitively, is where the business grows and where the future lies.

Your strategy is what will differentiate you from your competition, help the business weather difficult times, create long-term value for your shareholders, employees, and customers, and provide the roadmap to enable you to stay the course when times get tough, or change course due to changing economics or industry direction. When you consider succession and exit, the most important questions are:

- Is your strategy *sufficient* to deliver a profitable, sustainable business, now and in the future?
- Is your strategy compelling enough to attract and retain a strong team?
- Is your management team aligned to the strategy?
- Are they capable of executing it—profitably and sustainably?

Will your management team be able to recognize when a change in strategy is needed and have the ability to create a new more compelling strategy that they can execute?

Mark*, the owner of a well-respected sign* company, was confident in his strategy. He knew that the basis of their success was in gaining contracts with large growth companies that were expanding all over the country. With some urging, I encouraged him to do a strategic analysis, including a SWOT analysis, and to answer a series of strategic questions that can provide great insight for a leadership team. He recognized that the industries he had depended on upon, such as banks, which at one time were opening branches everywhere, were contracting now, shutting down locations as more people did their banking online and with mobile apps. He realized a new strategy was necessary and he needed his leadership team to embrace the need to rethink the direction they were headed.

Whether you are confident in your answers above or not, it's worth taking a fresh look at your strategy and your management team with an eye toward the company without you in it.

If your team cannot execute the strategy without you as owner/CEO, then either your management team is not adequately prepared yet, or your strategy is too complex. While the second reason is viable, most likely it's the first.

In a *Harvard Business Review* article, "Market Busting Strategies for Exceptional Business Growth"[12], powerful questions are posed that can complement a traditional SWOT analysis. We recommend using questions like these in your strategic planning process.

A compelling strategy can attract a top-flight offer from a third-party buyer. It can also influence the kinds of choices your management team makes on how to allocate resources to grow business value.

Tammy* had a great long-term business strategy for her design business. Her company was successful because it sold innovative design to major hotel chains and the opportunities were expanding as boutique hotels that valued the innovation mushroomed. The problem? Tammy planned to exit the business in sixteen months, and Tammy was the innovation leader *and* the chief salesperson. She had all of the relationships in the industry and she drove the creativity and innovation. Her leadership team was ill-prepared to take on those responsibilities, and it would take years before those skills could be developed within the core team.

Your strategic plan needs to be:

- *Sufficient* to deliver the profitability and sustainability you need.

- **Pared down to only what is *necessary*** to deliver the profitability you need. There is no need to add unnecessary work. We are all busy enough already.

- **Your leadership team must be *capable* of executing**—They must have the skills to do it—ultimately without your active involvement in the business.

- **With the *capacity* you have.** If your strongest leaders can do all of the work required to execute the plan, but it will require them working 100 hours/week to do it, you don't have the capacity.

We have worked with hundreds of organizations on building and implementing their strategic plan. Our process, mapped below, provides a framework to ensure these needs are met.

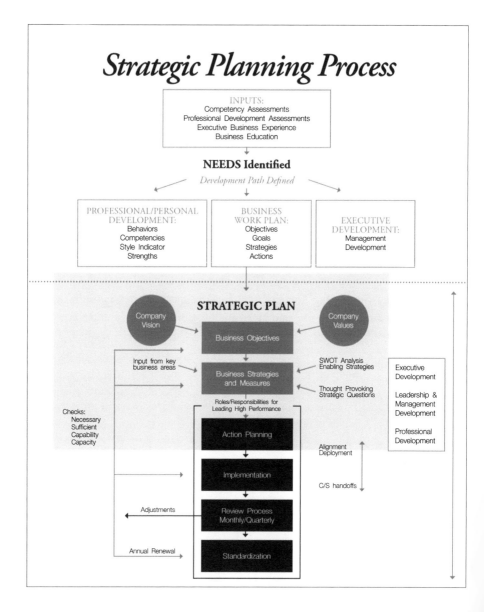

CHAPTER 7:

Intentional Development— Accelerating Management Performance

Your Management Team is typically one of the most important contributors to the value of your business, because in most cases, without a strong management team, you truly can't have a strong business. Your ability to build and execute strategy, run operations, deliver products and services, and manage the top and bottom line depends on upon your management team's performance. How ready is your team to run your business? How ready are they to run it without you?

We also know that your tendency will be to put this work off. You might be thinking, "I'm not going anywhere for 3–5 years; I don't need to worry about this." Well, first of all, you do.

Developing and grooming a successor or preparing your team to represent you in a viable business negotiation will require time. In fact, only 24 percent of high-potentials are leadership-ready.[13] They are not ready to take over the business. It takes time to develop managers for the level of responsibility and leadership required to run a business. Owners should expect to invest several years grooming a senior leader for a CEO role. Lower level roles will require a little less preparation time. If you plan to take a midlevel leader to CEO, you should plan for about five years of intentional development. If you are thinking you'll just hire the talent you need, not only is it expensive, but the right skills and experience with the wrong cultural fit can derail your entire process. What's more, starting in 2020, 40 percent of the workforce will be Millennials.[14] While they bring incredible talent, there are huge knowledge and capability gaps between them and the 25 percent of our workforce that will be over age 55.

No matter when you plan to exit, why wouldn't you invest in strengthening your managers now? It's a win-win; you get to reap the rewards of a strong team while you still own the business, and they are prepared for when you are ready to exit.

It's time to take a hard look at the managers in your organization and ask yourself if you really believe they have what it takes to run and grow your business. Can they represent it to a third-party buyer on your behalf? I know you want to say "yes" and affirm their capability. We all do. I mean, you hired and promoted many of them. But there is this nagging question about whether they could really manage and lead without you at the helm?

Too often, owners don't question—they assume their people are talented enough to achieve the goals. Or worse, are living on the hope that they will somehow get there, that they will be able to step up when the time is right. This works until reality sets in and they realize they are not confident or ready to trust their successor to take over. Sure, the selected successor may be talented enough. He or she may have all the right core competencies, but if the person has not adequately developed and applied those competencies, lacks experience using the competencies, or if sits on a highly dysfunctional team—or if your goals and the successor's goals are not aligned—then there is still development work that needs to be done.

Time and Budget

It's a common refrain to talk about money and time, and it's no different here. Finding the time for development and allocating budget for it are two identified challenges many leaders face.

Finding time is one of the most common and oft-used excuses at every level of the organization. I am not saying you aren't busy. I am saying that if it were urgent enough and important enough, you would find the time. It's the same thing with the budget.

As for accountability, it's a big thorn in most CEOs' sides. Nobody likes to badger, nag, or beat people up, and the phrase "holding people accountable" conjures up those images because most managers don't know how to hold their direct reports accountable. But accountability isn't about nagging, badgering, or beating people up. Done right, it is truly about setting very clear expectations for your leaders and then inviting them to live up to them. If they don't, your job is to understand why and to reduce or eliminate the barriers getting in the way.

Many CEOs do a poor job setting expectations for development and guiding their leaders through the process. If you want them to develop, you have to help them build a plan, expect them to learn and grow, and accept and encourage mistakes, failures, and discomfort—for both of you. So you need to be willing to take some risks so they can step outside their comfort zone and try some things. Smart risks, of course, but risks nonetheless.

The reality is the buck stops with you. So let's look at you:

Owner Independence: How Critical Are You to the Business?

Can you take off for a month or two, with very limited interaction with your management team, and have the confidence that your business will thrive in your absence and that any issues that come up will be handled effectively? Maybe not the way you would have handled them, but effectively? What about two months? Six months?

- ❏ Yes, of course!
- ❏ Maybe?
- ❏ Are you kidding me? I can't even take off for a full day without chaos ensuing!

If the answer is "Yes, of course," congratulations. You have achieved owner independence for your business. If the answer is anything less, you still play a critical role in the business—or at least you think you do.

It's important to distinguish between these two. If your management team is not capable of running the business for one, two, or six months without you, you do still play a critical role in the business. Sometimes we find that the management team can function just fine if the owner were to take off, but the owner is not ready or willing to let go. The owner's perception is that he or she is desperately needed in the business, so checks in regularly (or worse, won't take off) and invariably finds a way to "contribute," create a "need" or find a "crisis" to address.

Providing professional development for a leader is not an indication of weakness. It's an indication of growth potential for your successor and for the company. Development is an indication of high potential. Investing in poor performers or in a manager who has been promoted beyond his or her highest level of competence is typically not a good use of your resources. Development should be focused on those who have the potential to grow, to take on more responsibility, or to perform in their current roles even better. That's a good long-term investment for your business and for your successor.

When I worked for Procter & Gamble, they invested hundreds of thousands of dollars in developing me. They saw so much more in me than I saw in myself, and with quality training, coaching, targeted learning opportunities, and broadening experiences, I grew, took on more responsibility, and was able to make a much greater contribution to the company's bottom line. Your high-potential leaders can as well, but you have to make sure it happens and is planned in a way that delivers the return you need.

Assessing Performance

Talent Challenges

Changing demographics highlight additional challenges in developing strong C-suite leaders. The competition for skills and experience will continue to grow as boomer leaders retire and take their experience and knowledge with them and millennials are tapped to take on additional responsibilities. In addition, Millennials are constantly seeking new roles, new opportunities, and promotions. Engaging them in your business without a clear potential for growth opportunities, broadening experience, and promotions may result in much higher turnover—or worse—they stick around your company but get complacent.

Four Phases of Intentional Development

Let's take a look at the four phases of the Intentional Development Process and CARES.

We define CARES as the key factors for success in developing strong leaders: **Competencies, Attitude, Results, Experience, and Skills.** They are the key components for accelerating Management performance.

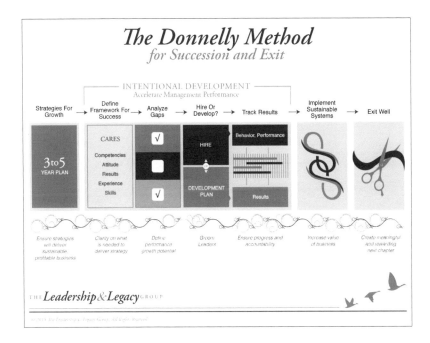

Define the Framework for Success

Building a development process begins with the question: How strong are your key leaders? It's not a simple question. You may have opinions about them, and they may be accurate, but the question is more about how strong are they in relation to these two critical gaps:

- Do they have the CARES (competencies, attitude, results, experience and skills) and capacity to execute your strategic plan, ensuring a profitable and sustainable business?

- Who will fill in the CARES gaps that will show up when you ramp down or exit the business?

If you've done the strategic planning, you know what work needs to be done to deliver the business results you want or need. Today, you know who is capable of delivering those results, but when you exit, not only do your skills and experience exit, the role and work allocation will likely need to change.

Each senior level role brings a set of critical and unique CARES to address the strategy and each role brings some CARES that are not being utilized in the business. Your Human Resources manager may bring operational skills which are not being utilized because he or she has a full-time HR job. If you pay attention to the breadth of CARES your employee base brings, you may find underutilized CARES that could be incorporated into the business. You may also be able to scale back and refocus some of the key roles so they target the key strategic areas in the business, instead of maintaining focus on ancillary work that has existed for years. Maybe some of the CARES your key people are investing in are not needed for your business success right now.

You'll also notice there are some areas that nobody brings CARES to cover. Either that part of your business strategy is not getting any attention, or someone is working really hard, outside their CARES area, to keep it afloat.

What happens when you exit? All those CARES that are crucial to executing those components of the business strategy that you uniquely contribute go away. Some of that slack might be taken up by a competent CFO, COO, or VP of Sales, for example, but who will do their work as they take over yours? It's possible that a lot of it will not be easily covered by anyone on the team. Might you have someone deeper in the organization who can begin to fill those gaps? Maybe, but if you've done nothing to prepare them to step in, they probably are not ready. Who is going to do it?

Several years ago, I watched a business owner giddy with excitement as he started taking off weeks at a time while his successor ran the business. The first few months, everything seemed to be going OK. But by the end of the first year, however, profits were down and the strategy execution was failing. By the end of the second year, the business was in the hole for over

$1 million. The owner realized he needed to step back in and lead. What were the gaps? There were gaps in operations that showed up as the business grew. The COO did not have the experience to address the infrastructure as the business grew. He was too focused on getting the product out the door. There were also gaps in the financials because the CFO only offered a traditional lens on the business, looking at line items and being very tactical with revenue and costs.

The impact of CARES gaps don't always show up right away, but with the right analysis of your strategy, and with careful attention to execution, over time, they can become very clear.

Analyze GAPS

Now that you understand the framework, it's time to take a look at your business.

Taking a broad-based review of the key roles and responsibilities required to execute your strategy is a good starting place. Not all senior roles are equal. The role components that are most critical for your organization will vary according to your strategy and business model. Filling those roles—or at least successfully executing those role components—will be critical.

For example, if your strategy requires expansion into new regions, your VP of Sales is key. If your strategy requires operational excellence, your COO role is probably key. You may have several roles or role components that are key. Another way to identify critical roles or role components is to ask which roles or job functions, if not done well, could take your business down?

It's not to say that other roles are unimportant, but they may not have risen to the level of critical.

If your company is small, you can start with an informal assessment of your organization, take your best cut at what CARES you need and then compare that to what you have today. Be sure to look at both CARES and capacity. If you have the CARES, but not enough capacity in some areas, you are going to have a gap that also needs to be addressed. Our recommendation is to first assess who in your organization already has the skills and competencies to close the gaps—even if they are not in that role right now. If there is no one, or there is but they don't have the capacity to take it on, because you can't pull their other work off their plate, then assess who else can be developed to close those gaps over time. If you don't have the skills and you don't have people who can develop those skills, recognize you will have to go outside the company to close the gaps. Doing this kind of gap analysis maximizes your utilization of development time and money because it is very targeted to what the business needs versus what you have to work with.

One of our clients set a goal to grow revenue by 30 percent. Their key strategies were expanding into new regions and getting more business from their existing clients. The current CARES gaps we identified included upselling to existing clients, scouting out the best new markets, and anticipating customer wants before their customers asked for them. For more than twenty years, the CEO had been the entire sales force. Expanding into new markets at the goal rate would tax his capacity already, *and* if he were to sell the business, he didn't have anyone on staff prepared to grow new sales.

You can hire skills needed to close the gap, or you can develop those skills. There is no correct answer. The key is that you are analyzing where development is needed and addressing it proactively.

I want to take a moment to make a distinction between *performance* and *potential*. Most organizations have leaders and staff who deliver exceptional performance but may never be able to take on more responsibility or perform well at a higher-level role. That's OK. We call them "Strong Performers at level." You want to keep them happy and engaged and they will consistently deliver great results. Some strong performers will continue to grow, and we designate them as "Strong Performers with high growth potential." You want to retain them too, *and* you want to invest in their development. Challenging them, growing them, and giving them opportunity will pay huge dividends. You may also have a few (hopefully very few) "Poor Performers." Before you let them go, figure out if they are in the wrong roles—due to a mismatch in personality, environment, skills or interest. Moving them into a new role or environment, or finding a better skills or personality fit can completely turn around their performance and pay off big for your company. If you find that you have a weak performer and you cannot turn them around using the methods above, you need to let them go.

Choosing to Develop vs. Hire

	High Growth Potential	At Level
STRONG Performer	They deliver exceptional results and they have high growth potential. Develop them, nurture them, and challenge them to grow to their full potential. If you don't, you could lose them to another challenging opportunity.	They do exceptional work in the role they are in and they enjoy the work. Keep them happy and engaged and they will deliver great results for the business.
POOR Performer	If you have a poor performer in their current role, role fit may be the issue. Once a right fit is found, growth potential may improve. On the other hand, they may simply be a poor performer. If so, help them find happiness elsewhere.	Help them find happiness elsewhere.

Developing your High Potentials and supporting your Strong Performers will not only pay you a strong ROI when you exit the business, it will also set you up to reap the benefits now as your team gains knowledge and experience that serves your business today, too.

You need to know who is ready to run your business profitably and sustainably now, and who will be ready in the future. If you are selling to a third party, you still should assess your staff because they will have to represent your business to a third-party buyer if you want to maximize your return. Plus, many private equity companies want to utilize your strong leadership team, and having one will help preserve their jobs and add value to your business.

Nobody is Ready

If nobody is ready, you need to assess *who can be ready* in three to five years.

When you put your top performers into the *right-fit* roles that have the greatest strategic impact, you move the business forward faster. Note the emphasis on right fit. Taking your top performing COO and making him/her the VP of Sales may not be wise—it depends on the skills and experience he or she brings. You might lose a top-performing COO and get a mediocre VP of Sales.

On the other hand, grooming a high-potential customer service manager to be the VP of Sales may be a brilliant move. Only you and your team can craft the right role and responsibility shifts. Thinking about role components instead of traditional roles can open up all kinds of possibilities for staffing and development. Maybe your top-performing COO can take on the interface between Sales and Operations with a dotted-line relationship from the sales team to the COO, freeing up your VP of Sales to focus more externally on market strategies and growth. Your sales team still reports to the VP of Sales, but they have an accountability matrix relationship to operations, ensuring operations can deliver what sales sells. Be willing to get creative with roles and reporting relationships.

An owner I once worked with had started his business thirty years prior, with three employees. Two of them were still with him and were holding C-suite roles. The VP of Sales had grown with the company and was performing well in his role. The COO, had not. The manufacturing systems were old and antiquated, the shop floor was disorganized, and efficiencies were low. One of his direct reports had been with the company only two years when he started showing signs of great promise. He organized the shop floor, streamlined the flow of products through the plant, and introduced a lean manufacturing mindset. Was he capable of running the entire manufacturing operation today? Possibly. Could he be capable in two years with the right intentional grooming? Absolutely. What to do?

Short-term, we recognized that the years of experience the COO brought were valuable to keep the operation functioning. We started with a conversation with the COO to gauge his commitment to growth if we supported him with targeted professional development. We laid out expectations for improvements in efficiency, and sent him to training for lean manufacturing, provided ongoing feedback, but in the end, the COO was not the right leader for what the business needed today. Over the next nine months, we assessed other roles he could fill that would be a benefit to the business and leverage his skills and experience, but unfortunately, the company was too small to offer many options. The owner gave him a small severance and helped him exit well. In the meantime, we developed his direct report and the owner promoted him to COO, where he embraced the opportunity to take the manufacturing operation to a whole new level. His success improved profitability and business value for the owner.

Analyzing your CARES and your allocation of roles against your strategic plan will not necessarily demand that you let anyone go, but it will likely highlight who has served you well in the past, who can bring strong leadership for your business, and who can lead in the future. You always get to decide what to do. The analysis process gives you data to help you more objectively assess. It can be hard and uncomfortable work. We recommend you do the assessment work and then decide how and when you want to take action. Knowledge is powerful, but you choose when and how to act on it.

We also know that if you move someone strong to fill a critical role or job function, you may simply create a new gap in their current duties. The daisy chain. You'll need to repeat the analysis process to evaluate who can backfill them. The daisy chain process can illuminate cross-training needs or strengths across the organization you didn't realize you had, as several people may be able to backfill roles. Or you may find that employees you already have can take on more responsibilities.

Of course, you may also decide through this process that it's right to bring in someone from the outside. If you do, we recommend defining your criteria for success in the role, critical job functions, specific cultural dynamics of your workplace, and then set up behavioral-based interviews with multiple people in your organization against those criteria. We also recommend a project-based interview process in which you ask your candidates to do a small, relevant project for you. This will provide insight into their thinking, their experience, their communications skills, and, if they do part of it on your site, how they interact with your team.

Going through this analysis process enables you to:

a.   Confirm that you have the right people in the right key roles *or* help you identify the changes you need to make

b.   Clarify your top performers and high potentials so you continue to groom and develop them for more responsibility

c.   Recognize the need to create stopgap measures to ensure business continuity in the short term, and identify candidates who could be developed into strong leaders for these critical business roles in the long term

This positions you for long-term success and provides growth opportunities for your team. We'll discuss how to groom your candidates for those roles shortly.

Raise Your Awareness

If this exercise has caused you to more fully recognize that you have employees who are not performing, and you've worked with them to help them learn, grow, and improve, but the results are not at the level you need, please give some serious thought to whether they belong in the role they are in. If not, can you find them another role in the company where they can contribute at a higher level? If so, finding a way to move them there can be a great benefit for your business and for them. If not, it may be time to help them find happiness elsewhere.

This is one of the biggest mistakes I find owners make. They can hold on to poor performers too long. Sometimes the business outgrows their capability. Sometimes they do not have the right mix of CARES for the role you need to have filled at this point in the lifecycle of the company. Sometimes they choose not to contribute at the level you need.

We've just done a top-down analysis of what it will take to deliver your strategy and how to cover the gaps that will arise upon your exit. Now it's time to invest in developing them—broadening their skills and experience and preparing them to take on increased responsibility.

Accelerator—Development Planning

When I talk to people about "development," they usually think I mean training. Certainly, training is a way to develop people, but it is just one of many ways. We are proponents of training, but we also recognize that traditional training is not the be-all and end-all for building capability and capacity.

We are strong advocates of using a wide range of development methodologies. Most people learn better when they learn through their own experience, so including intentional experiences through a variety of approaches including training, coaching, and mentoring, as well as identifying specific broadening experiences and targeting specific learning opportunities are all highly beneficial. It is also often softer on your budget. On our website, leadershiplegacygroup.com, you will find examples of some of the approaches that we use in our work with leaders. We typically use several methods to develop a set of skills and competencies, bundling them together to create a powerful growth curve for a high-potential candidate. While the methods may look like they are one-time events, they are not. They are a variety of reinforced activities and experiences done over time and built in collaboration with each other for maximum CARES-building, application, and reinforcement.

Take an example in which the gap analysis indicates a development opportunity in upselling the customer. Providing basic customer service training may be a good start, but it is insufficient. Add site visits to the customer's facility where your sales professionals can establish more direct productive relationships with the customer. Invite the senior leaders at the customer facility to a lunch 'n' learn roundtable to discuss ways your company can help them grow, with the philosophy that when your customers sell more, you sell more.

In that example, incorporating the roundtable, classroom training, site visits, and relationship building all reinforce each other. Any company can build in some of these generally inexpensive, highly effective methodologies for building capability and capacity. It simply requires some effort to do the gap analysis and lay out development options.

Development is not just about sending people to a training class on management or leadership. In fact, only 10 percent of their development should come from classroom training[15]. Development requires a more comprehensive approach that must incorporate intentional learning and experience, as well as actually delivering successful results. People need to be able to do the work, not just explain how the work should be done.

The key is to be intentional. Developing your team is an investment. This is critical because 37 percent of succession candidates fail.[16]

I love this quote:

> ## *"If You Think Hiring Someone, Training Them and Having Them Leave Is Expensive, Try Hiring Them, Not Training Them and Having Them Stay."*
>
> **Henry Ford, American Industrialist and Founder of The Ford Motor Company**

By simply investing in your people, you will create a huge advantage over your competitors, because most small businesses do little or no intentional development.

Development Plan

Building a development plan requires you to prioritize the particular skills and/or experience gaps you want to close and matching it to the most effective "Development Methodologies" for closing them.

An example: In banking, as in many businesses, it is really important that the CEO of a regional community bank has experience working with state legislators and regulatory agencies. The traditional approach would be to take your successor with you to meetings and conferences where they can get exposure to the key people and issues that are hot now. That's good, but insufficient. If you want your successor to be able to influence, you need to give them an experience of influencing. A stronger plan is to:

- Assign the successor the responsibility to select a relevant priority topic

- Prepare for a critical conversation with a key agency leader that will be of benefit to your organization.

- Set up the meeting for a few weeks out and then ask your successor to walk you through the preparation. In this process, you will learn

- Did he or she pick a topic that you think is worth investing in?

- Was his or her issue development, approach, and resolution directionally right?

- How successful your successor will likely be, and what areas could bite him or her?

- Whether you are confident your successor is ready to actually have the conversation?

- Provide targeted feedback on content, style, risk areas, mitigation, and potential outcomes.

- Depending on the status of his or her readiness, you may meet again to prepare. Your role would be to provide credibility and support in the conversation and be positioned to steer the conversation, if necessary.

- Send or accompany your successor to the meeting

- Debrief the meeting: What worked, and what didn't? What did the successor do well? What could be improved upon next time? What did the successor learn? What did you learn?

This is very different than "listening along."

Development methodology needs to be customized for each leader and each situation because each leader brings his or her own strengths, skills, learning styles, and experiences, and each situation has its own culture, environment, and risks. It must be built into the leader's schedule and reinforced consistently over time.

They key to building a solid development plan is incorporating development into the actual work of the leader and in alignment with business priorities and goals. This is a time to be creative! You have a business to run, so unless you have a highly technical certification or other need, it makes little sense to send your strongest candidates to training for weeks or months at a time. Use the opportunity to build in targeted learning experiences to craft a development plan that will enable people to learn, grow, and demonstrate the behaviors you need to see while they are running your business. This is a terrific win for your business and for them.

Retaining Your Top Performers/High Potentials

Investing in your people is a powerful retention tool.

Years ago, companies invested in a formal training and development process for their people, but with the rise of technology, the availability of training and education online has increased dramatically, and the economic pressures of profit and shareholder return have caused many companies to dramatically reduce their investment. In addition, many are worried that with our mobile workforce, they will invest in developing a strong performer and then lose him or her to the competition who paid nothing for the CARES development.

Unfortunately, they wrongly believe that they can get strong results without investing. In reality, owners can create substantial development opportunities while their employees are doing the work they are paying them to do—if they are intentional about it. Most of the methodologies we describe can be done while doing important work that delivers results. The methodologies just offer a more intentional and creative way of instilling new skills and experiences *while* the work of running the business is also being done. Sometimes, simply discussing career goals and expectations with your key employees will raise their performance. They know you are paying attention and you care about their success. Giving them opportunities, expecting more from them, those things don't have to cost much—time or money.

Do You Want Every Employee to Stay Forever?

What kind of question is that? Most CEOs I've worked with don't even consider this question, but it's an important one. You don't want every employee to stay forever.

1. Some are not performing today and should have been let go some time ago.

Holding on to employees who choose not to embrace change, or bring a poor attitude, or cannot or will not do what is required for their role in the business, is expensive and damaging to your culture. You need to pull the trigger and let them go.

2. Some are performing adequately today but will not be able to develop the CARES you need for the future.

There are times, as your business growth and strategic direction evolve, that you may also find that you have good people that no longer fit. The company has outgrown their CARES and they are no longer able to contribute at the level required. Or your culture may have changed under new leadership and they are struggling to adapt. This is a natural evolution and an opportunity to help your good people find happiness elsewhere.

For both of these categories, don't be afraid to pull the trigger; just get good HR counsel on how to do it right, with empathy for the individual(s), and to manage your corporate risk and exposure.

3. Some are hired for a specific purpose. We call them a "bridge" employee. When the particular work you hired them to do is done, so is their tenure with your company.

These people are usually hired with a timeframe in mind—interim positions, such as a fractional CFO or an interim president who will fill the gap until your son or daughter is ready to run the business.

Several years ago, Mark*, the owner of a $15 million company, decided he wanted more time to pursue his hobbies and other interests. His son, Tom*, the heir apparent, was not ready to take over and run the business and would not be ready for three to five years. Mark hired a president to run the business with the understanding that it was a short-term role and the president's bonus compensation at the end of the agreement would be based upon how profitable the business was at turnover and how ready Tom was to run the business. They put measures in place that would indicate Tom's readiness and created a simple formula for bonus pay. Because there was open conversation up front, and everyone knew the goals and expectations, it was a very productive and beneficial working arrangement for all.

4. Some are High Potentials who can learn and grow and take on increasing levels of responsibility.

They will be positioned to run your business, profitably and sustainably, and you want to keep them for a long time. These employees need to know there is a career path for them that will offer them continued growth opportunities that match their career aspirations. You need to have some confidence that they will stay. For these employees, you'll want to discuss your aspirations for them, their career development path, and in some cases, you may want to offer some "stay incentive." I suggest talking to experts in compensation to assess this for your business.

5. Some are Strong Performers who are at the top of their game.

They will continue to grow in their roles and take on challenges as they arise. They need to know their jobs are secure and their contribution to the business is critical. They need to be compensated well for the work they do and they need to have influence and autonomy to continue to do their best work.

In his best-selling book *Drive*, Daniel Pink identified three drivers for workplace satisfaction—purpose, mastery, and autonomy[17]. Employees who have an opportunity for all three will more likely stick with you for the long haul. Leadership changes can have a significant effect on these employees; as the culture changes, the opportunities change. You'll want to make sure your successor recognizes what motivates workplace satisfaction for these employees, is on board to support them, and has a good working relationship with them.

While your development plan and corresponding conversations are a good start, they may not be sufficient. Some sort of incentive plan may be in order. We mentioned this briefly for some of the categories above. You can explore incenting these employees with stock, perks/bonuses, deferred compensation, or life insurance value. Just remember, above about $75,000 income, money is not a strong motivator.[18] Opportunities to grow, to make a contribution and working in an environment of respect and appreciation are all much more important to the majority of employees, If you do decide on a financial incentive, we strongly recommend talking to a compensation expert who can help you evaluate which of these methods will work best for each of your key people, and how to structure it so it delivers the outcomes you want.

This comprehensive development lens provides the tools you need to build your top performing team that can run your business profitably and sustainably.

CHAPTER 8:

Implementing
Sustainable Systems

Every business has systems that the buyer will pay for. Yours does, too. The systems that are likely most valuable to your new owner are the systems that have the biggest impact on delivering sustainable profit and revenue.

It may be worth listing and assessing your particular systems to determine which are worth documenting, standardizing, and ensuring solid execution, if you have not done so already.

Systems that deliver profit and revenue in your business may include:

- **Strategy Development:** How do you develop your strategic plan and assess the implementation and effectiveness of that plan? Examples include: Annual strategic planning retreat, monthly review process, scorecard or dashboard systems.

- **Management Development Systems:** How do you develop your people so they can take on more responsibility and contribute more to the business? Examples include: Intentional development systems (See chapter 7), healthy culture systems.

- **Marketing Systems:** How you go to market, including everything from promoting your brand to prospecting, to networking. The systems that drive your sales pipeline. Examples include: brand promotion systems, prospecting systems, social media systems.

- **Sales Systems:** How you sell, including everything from getting the appointment to closing a sale. Examples include: Referral systems, pipeline tracking, sales meeting process, customer service.

- **Operational Systems:** How you move your product or service, including everything from the moment the sale is made to the moment of delivery to the customer. Examples include: manufacturing, quality control, technology/computer, distribution, product development.

- And of course, the foundation systems that support all of these—your **Financial Systems**. Examples include your accounts payable, accounts receivable, budgeting, financial reporting, audit systems.

To identify these for your business, ask what systems must be executed with excellence for your business to bring in revenue and be profitable. Everything you do in your business is defined by systems that can be flowcharted and assessed, from sweeping the floor to building a complex product. You need to identify which ones deliver the greatest value to your ideal buyer. For example, if you run a pharmaceutical business, your quality and material control systems are critical. It would be catastrophic for your business if you had to do a major recall for a control or quality issue. If you run an auto repair shop, your marketing systems, and your labor systems may be key. Without marketing, you become just another repair shop. If your labor systems are out of control, your business dies under the weight of your overhead. If you run an insurance agency, your sales and customer service systems may be most important. Once you gain a new client, they often become like an annuity. You don't have to re-up each client every year. You just have to keep the client happy.

Identifying Your Business Value Systems

Business Value Systems include systems that the buyer will gladly pay for. They may not assign a particular dollar value to them, but with them in place, you will get a higher valuation.

Here is a matrix of typical business value systems, the value impact and preliminary actions to take if that system is important in your business to deliver increased value. We advocate for hiring qualified experts in each of these areas.

Business Value Systems	Value Impact	Action Steps to Take
Financial Systems Cash flow, revenue, profitability, and clean financials.	Buyers want to know what the financial state of the business is. Clean financials instill confidence in the business. Confidence increases perceived value.	Consider hiring an auditing firm to do a review of your financials and clean up any areas at risk. If you are not profitable, work on that.
Strategic Planning Systems	Ensure you have a strategy that will carry your business into next decade.	Assess your strategy. (reference chapter 6).
Strong Management Team	Ensure you have a team capable of running your business profitably and sustainably. Explore confidentiality and non-compete agreements for key people.	Assess your team. Build your Intentional Development Process. (reference chapter 7).
Strong Customer Base and Customer Mix	Ensure customers are loyal to the corporation versus specifically to you or your people. Diversify your business so you reduce the risk to the company should you lose your "best client."	Build a plan to retain your best customers through the sale/transition. Add additional profitable customers to ensure one customer does not represent a significant portion of your business. Assess which customers are not profitable and consider letting them go now.

Business Value Systems	Value Impact	Action Steps to Take
Strategic Alliances, Referrals	Review strategic alliances and referral sources to understand what percent of business comes from these. If a lot, secure them for your new owner.	Make sure all agreements are legal and binding no matter who owns the business. Make introductions and build relationships for new owner.
Owner Independence	Begin transitioning major responsibilities for anything that depends upon you.	Develop your management team (reference chapter 7).
Product or Service Offerings	Review the products/services you sell. Assess profitability, growth potential, and competitive situation for each.	Assess whether your asset mix is serving your strategies, goals and profit priorities. Adjust your work accordingly.
Intellectual Property	If you have Intellectual Property, protect it. Consider areas that may not need IP protection but need confidentiality agreements.	Talk to an IP attorney if you have created anything unique in the business.
Brand Value, Goodwill	Assess your brand and value.	If significant, systematize the brand support systems.

Business Value Systems	Value Impact	Action Steps to Take
Physical Space	Assess what you own, what the company owns and what the business will need now and in the future.	Review lease agreement to ensure long-term viability of site, or ability to adjust or cancel contract with new owner.
Scale Potential	Assess which products or services have growth potential. Assess your systems for easy, fast, inexpensive scale to support the growth (outsource, add a machine, add a person, etc).	Put basic infrastructure in place to scale quickly.
Healthy Culture	Do a culture audit to determine areas of strength and whether there are any cultural dynamics that create significant business risk.	Develop CARES in your leaders that support the strengths in your culture. Reduce the areas of cultural risk.

What actions will you take to assess the internal systems that will make a difference in your valuation and attract the buyer you want?

The systems that drive your business are key to a successful transition. Invest in the most important systems.

A few pointers for investing in your key systems:

Document them: Create a flow chart of your key systems. Your flow chart should identify the critical steps in the process, who is responsible for them,

THE *Leadership & Legacy* GROUP

what success looks like at each step and how you measure success as that step is successfully completed.

Standardize them: Everyone should execute the system the same way. This increases efficiency and effectiveness. When someone finds a way to do it better, change the system and everyone does it the same better way.

Create in-process execution tools: Checklists, templates, forms, simple lessons, playbooks – all help ensure the systems will be executed as designed.

Track execution of each step and the results: If results are off-track, you should be able to go back through each step, looking at the tracking system to find out where the failure was.

With a basic systems infrastructure in place, you can create a more efficient, effective, reliable, sustainable, and profitable business. Select your key systems that will give you the biggest bang for the buck. Assess your operational needs and your saleable value options and get to work. It's worth it.

CHAPTER 9:

Get Sale-Ready Now

Will boning up on these assessed areas make your business more valuable? We can't say for sure, because your business is only as valuable as someone is willing and able to pay for it. We can say that without doing these things, you risk that there won't be anybody willing or able to pay what you think it's worth. Since you will leave your business one day, one way or another, it's important to get sale-ready so you are always prepared for a great opportunity or difficult life circumstances.

Whether your timeline is ten years or two, this work positions you to take advantage of unexpected opportunity—changes in the economy, strategic inquiries, industry changes. Whether your industry is expanding or contracting, being sale-ready enables you to sell at a better price as soon as you recognize there will be a contraction in the market, or hang on to the business for a higher price as the market expands. Options like this only benefit you if you are prepared.

Think about the last time you sold your house. When you decided to sell it, what did you do? You hired a landscaper to improve curb appeal. You hired a painter to freshen it up. You moved a bunch of stuff you'd been accumulating forever out to the trash or to Goodwill, and you kept the house show-ready nearly every day. If the house didn't sell quickly, you got to enjoy a beautifully landscaped, freshened up house. Well, it's the same analogy. If you invest in your leaders and your systems now, you'll benefit from it now, instead of waiting to spruce it up when you are ready to sell or exit, hoping someone will be ready to buy it from you right away. And, you'll likely get a better price than someone who just hangs a "For Sale" sign out.

Savvy sellers:

- Assess market trends to identify windows of time in the region that will give them a better return.
- Define key improvements to enhance the most important aspects of curb appeal: clean up the yard, give the interior a fresh coat of paint in neutral colors, repair anything that isn't working.
- Stage the house: Declutter, spruce up the look.

Most owners suddenly find their house much more attractive when they get it sale-ready and wonder why they waited to sell before investing.

The same applies to your business: Why not invest now and reap the rewards of running a well-functioning business?

For some owners, the house or business is in decent working order but the challenge is to find the sale opportunities. For this, I suggest what I refer to as being "Gym-Ready." You cannot predict when the right buyer will come along, and if you are planning a relationship sale, you cannot be sure exactly when your successor will "demonstrate the performance and competence" you seek. So, work on being "Gym-Ready" all the time. What do I mean by 'Gym-Ready'? Every morning before I start my workday, I make sure I have a gym bag fully packed and ready to go. I know I will not be able to get to the gym for a workout every day. Some days are booked solid and there is no space to fit it in. But my gym bag is in my car. Why? Because things change all the time. Schedules change. Opportunities show up in unexpected ways. If a meeting cancels or I get new information about an event I no longer want to attend, I am suddenly free to go to the gym! But if I don't have my gym bag with me, I probably won't get there. I would have to drive home, pack the bag and get back out to the gym. I may not have time and the opportunity would pass me by. More importantly, I may lose energy and motivation. Instead, I can fit in a workout because I am always "Gym-Ready."

What can you start today that will position you to be "Gym-Ready" when opportunity strikes?

Notes:

THE *Leadership&Legacy* GROUP

Section III:
Preparing for "What's Next?"

CHAPTER 10:

Don't Use Trial-and-Error

Leaving Your Business

We know that if you don't have an emotionally compelling "What's Next" to go to, and you don't have confidence you are going to get the financial return you want or need for your retirement as it stands today, you are not going to leave your business. Oh, you may say you are going to leave. You may even promote someone to be president and begin conversations about financing a buyout. You might even start taking more time off, playing some golf on Wednesday afternoons and Friday mornings. You might take a few extra weeks off to see grandkids or hike the Grand Canyon. But when you come back, you will invariably insert yourself into the business and muck up (or rescue) the company from the clutches of your appointed successor.

Whether he or she is performing admirably or poorly, your insertion into the business will not only be a distraction for the company; it will also create stress and uncertainty across the organization as everyone from president to newest employee wonders who is really in charge and what weight they carry. You can undo years of value-added work in the blink of an eye as your body language reveals your support or lack thereof for the work of the new "designated" leader. So, you need to ensure that you have your emotionally compelling "What's Next" clearly defined—for their sake.

But there are other really good reasons to invest in defining your emotionally compelling "What's Next." Investing in that is important if for no other reason than it will keep you motivated, engaged, and healthy.

Having an emotionally compelling "What's Next" provides meaning, purpose, and fulfillment in ways that you used to get from work, but without the same kinds of pressure and responsibility. It's kind of like being a grandparent. You get to have fun with your grandkids, play, give them ice cream and chocolate, but then, when it gets late or they begin to get cranky, you send them home with mom and dad and you go on enjoying your life. That's what having an emotionally compelling "what's next" is like, but you don't necessarily spend all day with the grandkids. You spend the time and energy you want doing the things that bring you purpose, meaning, and fulfillment. What's not to love about that?

In this section, we're going to look at the factors that matter most in planning for your own meaningful and rewarding next chapter.

Preparing for a Meaningful and Fulfilling "What's Next?"

Years ago, workers expected to retire, sit in a rocker, move to assisted living, and then pass on. Today, fortunately, that is not the case. So, this generation of business owners has the blessing of time and the curse of figuring out what will keep them engaged in life and in the community in a meaningful way. Companies are taking notice as AARP launches a new website, Life Reimagined, and Encore.org (formerly Civic Ventures) launches a book and model to encourage Encore Careers consisting of meaningful giving back.

Trial-and-Error Never Worked in Business; Why Would You Use It to Discover Your "What's Next?"

Programs like these often encourage you to try out things that "interest" you, often recommending you volunteer for a nonprofit or a community organization you like or do consulting in your area of expertise. Because they are "trials," there is little planning or intentionality as to how your strengths will be used, or what about that nonprofit or community organization deeply inspires you. Working with a nonprofit or community organization can be inspiring if the fit is right. It can be a huge drain if the role fit is wrong, potentially leading to disappointment, frustration and disengagement.

Furthermore, while volunteer work can be inspiring, it is not right for many business owners. Many owners still want to or may need *to work*.

Just like in business, where there are proven methodologies for growing your business, building a strategic plan, increasing operational efficiency and more, we have built *a proven process for discovering your meaningful and rewarding "what's next?"*

For baby boomer business owners, this transition is particularly significant.

Why? Because the majority of business owners have their identity tightly tied to their business. The problem is that when it's time to exit, it's incredibly difficult to unhook. Mentally, emotionally, physically, and even spiritually. Let's take a look.

Mentally Hooked

As an owner, founder, CEO, you have been the one in charge, the big kahuna, the top dog, the "buck stops here leader". Running a business is mentally stimulating. It can be exhausting and stressful, of course, but there is always an opportunity or challenge to keep you engaged. What will keep you mentally engaged after your exit?

Emotionally Hooked

This is all about identity, status, and self-worth. Most owners have their identity tied to their business. Whether you were the founder, grew up in it, or bought it from a previous owner, this became your baby. Whether you acknowledge it or not, your life has been built around the expectations and demands of the business. If the business needed your undivided attention, you gave it. If the business required an infusion of capital, you found it. Whatever was required, you delivered to the best of your ability. Your life has also benefited greatly from the business. You were in charge of your own destiny. The business supported your family and your lifestyle, as well as the families of all your employees. Your business may have played a visible role in the community or in your industry. Your business provided resources and an economic impact.

When you show up in the community, in your industry, or at your office, you are not just Mr. Smith. You are Mr. Smith, CEO, owner of XYZ company, employer of many, person with the ability to write a check, person who can fire, hire and promote, person who can make or break a career, person who can influence community choices, legislation, and even other business and community leaders. It's part you and part your position in the business and community.

When you relinquish that role as the CEO/Owner of…", who are you? Without the title, the resources, the same level of influence, you have to redefine who you are. Your status changes, because your influence and access to resources change.

Often, when people ask retired owners/CEOs about what they do, their response is defined by what they "used to do"—who they used to be. "I am the former CEO/Owner of…". And then I often hear that followed by a whole lot of explanations about how successful their business was or how they navigated a successful sale or how they are still involved in the business in some capacity.

Physically Hooked

Let's face it. Your habits of going to work by 7:30 a.m. every day have been ingrained in you for years. Ending that physical habit is tough. When your emotional energy is invested in the business, and your mental energy is in the business, it's very difficult to disconnect physically as well.

One of my clients turned his business over to his son and told his son he only planned to come in two days each week. They agreed the father would come in on Mondays and Wednesdays and they carved out a role for him that would add great value to the business and could be done well in that period of time. The father/owner was very excited about his newfound freedom and confident in his son's ability to lead. Until Tuesday. When he woke up feeling lost. What do I do? So, he went into the office…just for a little while. Then it happened again on Thursday. Week after week, he struggled to break the physical pattern. His energy was in the business and his habits were in the office.

On the other hand, you may notice reductions in your stamina and a reduced commitment to work so many hours and so hard. That's OK. You've earned the right to shift your hours and work a 40-, 20-, or zero-hour work week. If you can navigate the emotional aspects of that, the physical can follow.

Spiritually Hooked

You may or may not feel that your business has been a "Calling," as Gregg Levoy describes it, in his book, *Callings:* "A calling may be to do something (change careers, go back to school, have a child) or to be something (more creative, less judgmental, more loving)."[19] If your calling has been to build this business, good for you. Now you must discern what is next for you. If your calling has *never* been to build this business, good for you! Now you must discern what your calling really is and take the opportunity to pursue it.

Why Discerning Your Calling Is So Important Now

Allowing your next chapter to simply unfold leaves you at risk. You disconnect from what has been such an important part of your life for so long. You lose your connection to community. You disengage from a daily routine and in many cases, a purpose—even if that purpose was to support your family and the families of your employees. Many CEOs experience bouts of depression. They eat too much, drink too much, sit too much in the first six to twelve months after retirement. And the older you are, the more difficult the recovery is. Once those habits get ingrained, it's harder to stop them.

Your Well-Defined Role

You don't need to leave because I urge you to, of course, but you can't stick around your business without a clearly defined role and responsibilities. You will get in the way of the management team you just developed to run it without you. If you have no ownership in the business, you have no business hanging around. If you have some ownership still in the business, you need a well-defined role and boundaries, whether it's as an employee or a consultant.

The beauty of a transition like this is that you get to decide. You decide when you want to activate an exit or ramp-down of responsibilities. You decide what role you want to play. You decide how long you want to stay. *You decide.*

Because of that I strongly—and I mean *strongly*—recommend going through a discovery process to plan your next chapter *before* you exit your business. Don't become a health statistic. Plan your next chapter within twelve to eighteen months of your exit. It's critical.

CHAPTER 11:

Executive Transition Can Be a Very Exciting Time

Executive transition can be a wonderful and rewarding time! A time to create a new emotionally compelling identity.

If you plan it right, you can craft something that will be more invigorating than maybe anything you have ever done. Unfortunately, most executives don't think it's necessary to plan. We do. We've seen the outcomes when executives take the proverbial "six months off just to see what happens." They lose their connection to work, to business, to the many communities that they were once an active and vibrant part of.

We know that without a plan, you will likely fall into a state of disillusionment as your patterns, habits, and community changes. Your spouse will be affected as well.

Start your executive transition at least one year to eighteen months before your planned exit date. The process will likely take you six or nine months, and we recommend you complete it before your exit so you can ramp down work demands while ramping up the lifestyle changes you want to make.

When you have a well-defined "What's Next?", it's much easier to move forward.

Our "What's Next?" process begins with uncovering three components:
- Your favorite strengths—those you love to use.
- Your passions—what wakes you up every morning excited about the day ahead.
- Your particular lifestyle priorities at this stage of your life.

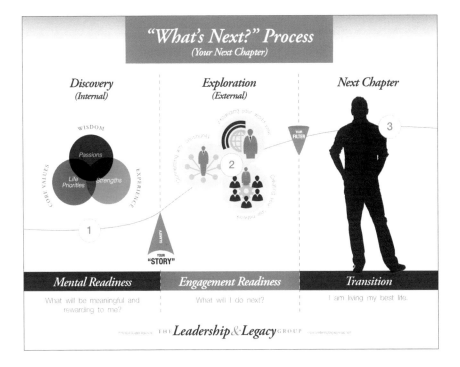

"What's Next?" Process
(Your Next Chapter)

Discovery (Internal) — Exploration (External) — Next Chapter

Mental Readiness — Engagement Readiness — Transition

What will be meaningful and rewarding to me? — What will I do next? — I am living my best life.

THE *Leadership & Legacy* GROUP

We know that the people who are most fulfilled invest in doing things they are passionate about, in ways that make them feel good about themselves, facilitate great outcomes, and fit with the lifestyle important to them now.

While this process is best done with the help of an Executive Coach or Career Coach who brings deep expertise in leadership, business, and personal transition, we will provide you with some simple exercises to get you started. We want to stress that this is a process. It's about self-reflection, introspection, exploration, discovery, validation, and then refinement. In the end, you will have the framework to create a truly meaningful and rewarding "What's Next?"

What Are You Passionate About?

Most owners tell me they have no idea what they are passionate about. That's OK. I can assure you—you do have passions, and we have the tools to uncover them.

Maybe yours are not the kind that make you jump up and down, giddy with excitement. That may not be your style, but you do have themes—core areas that motivate you emotionally. Maybe it's the thrill of adventure or the competitive win, or maybe it's a particular hobby you want to excel at, like soccer or hunting small game. Maybe it's leading a diverse team to tackle a complex challenge, or securing financing for bringing more comprehensive arts to your community, or growing a talented workforce. These categories are just scratching the surface. When you are done with this process, you can define specifically what you are passionate about. For example, one client discovered he was passionate about: *"I love designing and orchestrating a strategic vision—a grand idea!"*

Some owners tell me they already know what they are passionate about, but they insist it's never going to help them with their next chapter. They say it can never be a focus area for the next phase of their life.

For example, one owner told me he was passionate about basketball, but he can't play ball (he's too old, too tired, too easily injured), he can't coach ball (can't travel, too many late nights, no interest in fighting angry parents or fans, and he doesn't have the energy for the intensity of the weekly games), and he can't referee.

I assured him, watching basketball on TV may be the way that this passion comes to life for him now, but that does not mean that there aren't components of that passion that can be ignited in other activities or "work." There are many ways our true passions can manifest. In our work together, we uncovered that his passion around basketball was truly about the engagement of a team. That can be applied to much more than basketball. In fact, he got involved leading an innovative workforce development program that combined education and skills-building through team sports.

The key is to not to hook into the immediate opportunities that sound interesting. Clients who do this often come to regret it. Instead, uncover them through a structured process of reflection, looking across your life. You are pulling together themes and connections that will engage you and provide an opportunity to bring value to people and organizations that matter most to you.

Exercises to get started:

1. What accomplishments are you proudest of over the course of your life?

_____

_____

_____

2. What activities have really engaged you? What did you enjoy most about them?

_____

_____

_____

3. What did you love to do when you were a child? What specifically was so meaningful to you?

_____

_____

_____

Yours are there; we just need to tease them out.

Let's see how this dovetails with Defining Your Favorite Strengths.

Combine Your Passions with Your Favorite Strengths

Most owners nearing retirement age grew up at a time when we didn't pay much attention to what is now known as Positive Psychology. We just worked hard and kept our noses to the grindstone. Today, based on years of research in this new field, according to Gallup, we know that there is infinite potential in developing what is *right* with people versus fixing what's innately "wrong" with people.[20] We define *strengths* as an individual's ability to consistently provide near-perfect performance in a specific task. We have consistently found that when employees know and use their strengths, the effect on individuals, teams, and organizational performance is spectacular.

Employees who use their strengths every day are *six times* more likely to be engaged than those who do not.'[20]

It's a paradigm shift, but a good one as the research is very compelling.

Strengths may include competencies, attitude and skills from the CARES model (chapter 7), as well as qualities, traits, attributes, and characteristics that you either do naturally well, or have built the ability to do well over time. They can include tangible skills, such as the ability to sink a high percentage of free throws, to qualities such as compassion or tactfulness, to characteristics such as being able to start a conversation with anyone. They contribute to your uniqueness—making you, you.

Unfortunately, most of us do not have a good sense of what our strengths are—what we are best at. Our workplaces are terrific at telling us directly or indirectly what we do *not* do well, and our own internal voice reinforces that. I am always amazed at how many owners have no idea what they are good at, beyond the broad categories of "selling" or "taking risks." They often take for granted the unique strengths they have, assuming everyone can do those things well. They attribute much of their success to either hard work—just persistently keeping at it—or a particular set of skills they worked hard to develop, such as making deals, financial analysis, strategic thinking. They may even attribute it to luck. It is rarely any one of those, and usually a combination. Honing in on the particulars, whether innate and developed or built by brute force, can open up boundless opportunities to make an impact.

When I am presenting to an audience on this topic, one of my favorite exercises is to ask them to reflect back on a time in their career when they were working in an area of weakness. A time when they did not have the strengths required to do the job well. How did they feel? Usually, I hear words like, hopeless, ineffective, embarrassed, frustrated. How were their results? Poor, adequate, marginal. Then I ask them to reflect back on a time when they were working in an area of strength—they were good, and they knew it! How did they feel? Confident, competent, capable, in control. How were their results? Excellent, strong, stellar, solid. So as you enter this next phase of life, which do you want? (Rhetorical question, of course!)

But our "American Dream" culture does not invite us to celebrate our strengths openly. Instead, it pummels us with reminders of our weaknesses. The truth is, we need to know what we are best at, now more than ever, because those things we do well make for easy work and more fun. At this stage in your life, you have earned the right to select "work" that is easy and fun—for you—and it can still make a profound impact. Defining and articulating our strengths will not give us a fat head. Arrogance and bragging about them might.

One client identified this as one of his favorite strengths:

I've been successful getting in and figuring out what needs to be done to work across different entities to build or rebuild an entire organization to create something powerful and often transformational.

Wow! This is a strength set that many different organizations would love to have access to.

There are several ways to begin to hone in on your unique strengths.

Exercises:

1. Certainly, you have received feedback, formal and informal, direct and indirect, throughout your career and life. Reflect on performance reviews from your favorite roles, feedback from your favorite boss, colleague, or sports coach. Review any testimonials that others have

offered you. Pull out old assessments you've taken. All of those give you clues to your strengths.

_____

_____

_____

2. You may have also identified your own strengths as you went through life and work, noting things that just seem to come easily to you or areas where you had to work hard but consistently delivered strong results.

_____

_____

_____

3. Ask five trusted friends or colleagues. You need to trust them because you have to believe their input. Contrary to conventional wisdom, they do not have to know you well. It's amazing how quickly and well others can see us.

_____

_____

_____

Take some time to identify what your most enjoyable strengths are and incorporate those into your discovery process.

Lifestyle Priorities

When you are making major changes in your life, a new job, a move to another city, a marriage or divorce, it's an opportunity to take stock of everything in your life. Take stock of the habits and patterns you've built. Which are serving you and which are carryovers from a different era? Take stock of the things you have and the things you don't. Do they match what matters most now? Take stock of the people you spend your time with and the activities you do outside of work. Take stock of the activities you never find time to do. Are they important enough to build into your life now?

When I exited Procter & Gamble years ago, I was exhausted. For fourteen years, I had worked 60+ hours/week, logged over forty-two weeks of plane travel for four of those years, including many international trips. It took a toll on me, and when I left, one of my lifestyle priorities was not to start my work day before 8:30 a.m. I needed sleep! Another was to design my work and life so that travel was *my* decision, not the customer's or employer's decision. I wanted to decide when I would travel and when I am home. Today, my business could take me all over the world, but it doesn't. I do most of it within a fifty-mile radius of my house.

What about you? What are you ready to give up?
What do you want to embrace?

Many owners tell me they want to travel, spend time with family, and play a lot of golf. I can tell you that those activities are wonderful, and in six months, you'll be bored.

In this section, we want to assess the most critical lifestyle priorities for you now.

Exercises:

1. Whom do you want to spend your time with?

_____

_____

_____

2. What cultures or environments feed you—where you feel your best?

_____

_____

_____

3. What do you want to ensure there is time for? What personal priorities matter?

_____

_____

_____

Those kinds of questions begin to get at the lifestyle that is most important.

I want to say a few words about "work." You may or may not be looking for paid work. I am going to use the word "work' to mean meaningful activities that engage you for purpose and intent, whether paid or not. It's your choice whether you want to collect a consulting fee, a salary, or some other form of compensation. That is independent of what provides "meaning" for you.

Putting It All Together

Now that you have the three components identified, we recommend you craft a compelling communication—your *story* of who you are now and what you want to contribute. You want to be specific on your passions and strengths and broad on where and how to invest them.

Example:

I love designing and orchestrating a strategic vision – a grand idea – or being invited in on a vision because I am the person who can see how it can be done and can lead the accomplishment of something amazing. My colleagues have consistently called upon me because they know I can see the inherent potential in the bones of an organization and assess the resources available to address the inherent challenges. In fact, I thrive in complex situations where the risks are high, there are many competing priorities and it requires alignment across a diverse group of people or organizations to build the infrastructure, lay the foundation and ultimately, achieve something big and transformational. I see what people are capable of and know how to create an environment where they can access resources they need and flourish.

You'll need a few more sentences to create the power story that will help you connect with the right people and opportunities, but this should give you a sense of what it might look like. Armed with your power story, it's time to get out there and start talking to people you know, people who intrigue you and people they know. By strategically building your network of relationships, sharing your power story, asking for advice and input, and refining your direction, you *will begin to move towards the people, organizations and specific opportunities* that will bring meaning for you and make the kind of contribution you want.

I wish you much continued success!

Abby

Action Steps for Implementing the Donnelly Method:

_____

_____

_____

_____

_____

_____

_____

_____

_____

_____

THE *Leadership* & *Legacy* GROUP

Action Steps for Planning Your 'What's Next?':

_____

_____

_____

_____

_____

_____

_____

_____

_____

_____

_____

THE *Leadership & Legacy* GROUP

THE *Leadership&Legacy* GROUP

Ready To Get Started?

Visit our web site www.leadershiplegacygroup.com **for video, audio, blog posts and more**

What We Do at The Leadership & Legacy Group

Our clients are business owners like you, who have invested 20, 30, even 40 years building their business and recognize the importance of proactively planning for an eventual exit. Call us if you want to talk about:

STRENGTHENING MANAGEMENT PERFORMANCE
We ensure you have the leadership in place to run and grow your business, profitably and sustainably. Whether you stay another 15 years or plan to exit in two, you need a strong team to ensure you get the return on your investment.

PLAN YOUR 'NEXT CHAPTER'
We help you create a lifestyle that is meaningful and rewarding for you as you move into the next phase of your life. We co-create the roadmap for an engaging and fulfilling 'Next Chapter'.

If you are ready for a confidential conversation about your business, contact us!

Abby Donnelly, Founder of The Leadership & Legacy Group
Abby@LeadershipLegacyGroup.com
Office: 336.458.9939

Visit www.SuccessionPlanningRoundtable.com for information on events local to the Piedmont Triad, NC and articles such as:
- Six Critical Questions Every Business Owner Should Answer
- The Seven Secrets to Preparing For Succession

Visit www.StraightTalkAboutSuccession.com for more tools and to purchase books in bulk. We offer a 10% discount if you order more than 10 books. 20% discount for more than 20.

THE *Leadership & Legacy* GROUP

About the Author

Abby Donnelly is the Founder of The Leadership & Legacy Group and an expert on the leadership side of succession planning and exit. She works closely with business owners and CEOs to strengthen their management performance and develop the leaders they need to run and grow their business. She also works one-on-one with executives to facilitate the discovery of a meaningful and rewarding Next Chapter.

A fourteen-year veteran of Procter & Gamble, Abby led improvements in leadership effectiveness, productivity, and streamlined business processes. She was a partner at Sandler Training, a franchise specializing in sales and sales management training, for more than eleven years. She is a graduate of the University of Florida and holds a Master of Statistics.

Abby founded the Succession Planning Roundtable, a forum that draws local experts to share experiences and lessons learned on succession planning and exit. She is a certified speaker for Vistage International, an organization of CEOs, speaking on "Why Most Succession Plans Fail," and is the Chair of the Greensboro Chapter of the Women Presidents' Organization. Abby has been featured in the Triad Business Journal and is a renowned Triad-area speaker on improving performance.

Abby is the internationally recognized author of *The Networking Works!*, a book and training curriculum on strategies for building a strong professional network and *128 Tips to Make you a More Effective Leader.*

Abby serves on several boards including First Bank (formerly Carolina Bank), Kindermusik International, the Greensboro Chapter of the Society of Financial Service Professionals and Crescent Rotary Club.

To contact Abby to purchase multiple copies of this book or to book her as a speaker, e-mail Abby@LeadershipLegacyGroup.com, or call 336-458-9939. More tips and techniques on this topic are also available at www.StraightTalkAboutSuccession.com.

References

1   Finnel, K. O. *The ESOP Coach: Using ESOPs in Ownership Succession Planning.* Executive Financial Services, 2010.

2   Business Enterprise Institute, Inc. Business Owner Survey Report, 2014.

3   Ungashick, Peter. *Dance in the End Zone: The Business Owner's Exit Planning Playbook.* Alpharetta: BookLogix, 2013.

4   Leonetti, John M. *Exiting Your Business, Protecting Your Wealth: A Strategic Guide for Owners and Their Advisors.* Hoboken, NJ: John Wiley & Sons, 2008.

5   Exit Planning Institute. State of Owner Readiness Survey, 2013.

6   https://www2.census.gov/programs-surveys/susb/tables/2012/us_state_totals_emplchange_2011-2012.xls

7   Beckhard, R., & Dyer, W. G. (1983). Managing change in the family firm—Issues and Strategies. Sloan Management Review, 24, 59-65.

8   Applegate, J. *"Keep Your Firm in the Family."* Money, January 1994, 88-91.

9   Dyer, W. Gibb. *Cultural Change in Family Firms: Anticipating and Managing Business and Family Transitions.* San Francisco: Jossey-Bass, 1986.

10 Exit Planning Institute. Powerpoint presentation: "Connect-Discover-Empower, Pathways to Effective Exit Planning," 2013.

11 Names and industries have been changed to protect the privacy of the individuals I have worked with.

12 McGrath, Rita Gunther, and Ian C. McMillan. "Market Busting Strategies for Exceptional Business Growth" *Harvard Business Review.*

13 UNC Executive Development & Human Capital Institute. *How to Accelerate Leadership Development.* University of North Carolina Chapel Hill Leadership Survey, 2014.

14 Asghar, R. *What Millennials want in the workplace (and why you should start giving it to them).* Forbes. Accessed November 13, 2016. http://www.forbes.com/sites/robasghar/2014/01/13/what-millennials-want-in-the-workplace-and-why-you-should-start-giving-it-to-them/

15 https://www.trainingindustry.com/wiki/entries/the-702010-model-for-learning-and-development.aspx

16 Leonard, David. *"Putting Success Back in Succession Planning: The Role of Learning and Development."* Ideas@Work, UNC Chapel Hill Kenan-Flagler Business School 1 (2011): 26-36.

17 Pink, Daniel H. *Drive: The Surprising Truth about What Motivates Us.* New York, NY: Riverhead Books, 2009.

18 Kahneman, D., and A. Deaton. *"High Income Improves Evaluation of Life but Not Emotional Well-being."* Proceedings of the National Academy of Sciences 107, no. 38 (2010): 16489-6493. doi:10.1073/pnas.1011492107.

19 Levoy, Gregg. *Callings: Finding and following an Authentic Life.* New York: Harmony Books, 1997.

20 Gallup Inc., http://www.centerforstrengths.com/employee-engagement/